YOUR LAST BOOK TO FAST FINANCIAL FREEDOM

Financial Freedom is EASY.
Whatever you heard before was 100% WRONG.

ARYAN CHAUDHARY

FiNGERPRINT!

Published by

FiNGERPRINT!

An imprint of Prakash Books India Pvt. Ltd.

113/A, Darya Ganj, New Delhi-110 002,
Tel: (011) 2324 7062 – 65, Fax: (011) 2324 6975
Email: info@prakashbooks.com/sales@prakashbooks.com

facebook www.facebook.com/fingerprintpublishing
twitter www.twitter.com/FingerprintP
www.fingerprintpublishing.com

ISBN: 978 93 5440 362 0

Processed & printed in India by HT Media Ltd, Greater Noida

Your Last Step to Fast Financial Freedom

is the easiest and the most realistic, strategic roadmap to turn your knowledge and dreams into lifelong income regardless of your current financial situations. It's a book for generations to create generational wealth over a period of time.

Aryan Chaudhary

DEDICATION

To,

my mother, who always covered me,
stood by me, and supported me;

my father, who took care of me and taught me real honesty;

my elder brother, who always put me first in his world and
has been there every single second to solve my problems;

my two lovely sisters, who shaped me by beating me in
my childhood (I know you'll read it!);

all my lovely kids—Arnav, Aditi, Ayati, Arjun,
Vansh, Shreya, and Lakshya;

my teachers and trainers, who taught me how to keep
fighting and become a leader;

leaders, marketers, and entrepreneurs, who shaped my work
life and who have been my inspiration;

and my friends;

I can't thank you all enough for what I am today.

Contents

ACKNOWLEDGEMENTS

First of all, I want to thank God for putting me through rough times in life so I could fall, get up, and fight for what I deserved.

Then I would start giving very special thanks to the people who introduced me to the concept of financial freedom, even though I did not understand it well at the age of sixteen. Thanks to Amway, Forever Living, Ebiz, T-Harv Eker, Tony Robbins, and Robert Kiyosaki.

I would also not forget to thank people who have betrayed me, cheated me, and stolen from me. If you wouldn't have done that I wouldn't have started a new life again, and again. So, thank you for everything.

WHAT IS THIS BOOK ABOUT AND WHAT IT'S NOT

─────── ▲ ───────

Before we begin, you need to have a clear understanding of what this book is about and what it's not.

This book is about raising you from ground zero to the top by understanding the secret game of money.

This book is about roots and not about the leaves.

This book is about creating a super strong foundation for your financial freedom.

This book is about being laser-focused on your dreams, mindset, action plans, skill sets, income with less work and high returns, spending, investing, art of accumulation, and being debt-free.

This book is about controlling your financial future, your financial destiny, and creating generational wealth regardless of your current financial situation. Even if you are broke, you can still make it. Have faith and follow the steps.

This book will be your playbook for fast financial freedom.

Being financially 'free' can save so many lives—it can bring happiness to your kids, parents, siblings, your partner, and a whole lot of other loved ones around you. Imagine the impact you can make on the lives of your most loved ones, as well as the ways in which you can impact the society.

INTRODUCTION

———— ⌃ ————

I was introduced to the word 'financial freedom' by some famous multi-level marketing companies when I was a teenager, and I hardly understood the game behind it.

Since then, I have sold stuff worth many millions ranging from notebooks, diaries to martial art training programs, T-shirts to medicines, real estate to weight loss packages. I have sold marketing services, sales training workshops, and built my own company, starting from a huge debt to accumulating $2 million in six months with a small team of four members. In my early twenties, I was a millionaire but I lost it all. I recovered soon and once again became a millionaire. But I went bankrupt again—five times in all—because I didn't understand money and its secret domination rules.

Later on, I realized that I was amazingly good in marketing and sales, but somehow I couldn't get that word financial freedom out of my mind. During the twelve years of my struggle, I went bankrupt five times in a span of seven years. Ultimately, I found that the only solution to all my money problems was financial freedom, but the big question was how?

Going back to my bad times and worst nightmares, every time I went bankrupt, I recollected what made me bounce back financially. What I did to earn money again and again. The answer to that big question was marketing strategies.

Yet, I still didn't know how to become financially free and live the life of my dreams. But as a marketing strategist I created a strategy and found that financial freedom was the easiest thing, only people didn't know it—which is also not their fault because they have been guided to run in the wrong direction. If a doctor gives you wrong medicines, it's not your fault. As a patient, you only look up to your doctor, and, in this case, financial gurus.

The second thing I found out was that all those so-called financial freedom gurus were not touching the roots or core problems; they were just repeating the same old stuff, and their talks produced nothing in results; it only made *them* money and only *they* became financially free and not their followers.

The third thing I found out was that they had been teaching *how* you could be financially free and not *what* would make you financially free. They didn't give a proper blueprint, and that's why I was stuck. But I found it out by myself, and now it will be available for you as well. Just the way half-cooked food can never taste perfect, the same way *some* useful but incomplete knowledge can never give you 100% results.

I am ready to share all these secrets with my readers and some more secret strategies that will change the game in your life for now and forever.

Go through this book slowly and carefully and you will discover how easy it is to be financially free. I was overwhelmed looking at the book indexes of famous gurus so I didn't even read them. One thing I promise that this book won't do is overwhelm you; in fact, it will show you a crystal-clear path to your financial freedom and once you finish the book, there will be a surprise bonus for you.

The purpose of this book is to transform as many lives as possible and help them to live tension-free, financially.

THE TWO KINDS OF PEOPLE

There are two kinds of people who will read this book and if you are reading this, you, most probably, fall in the first category. For you, I have to say this: **what you are seeking is seeking you.**

In order to achieve financial freedom and control your financial destiny, your current life status depends on whether you are serious or casual, whether you are a fighter or a quitter, whether you are a lion or a rat, whether you are a producer or a consumer, whether you are an executer or a shirker, whether you come up with results or reasons, whether you care about your family or you take it easy . . . And when you take your finances easy, then your life will be extremely hard on you, remember that.

I want to tell you that being financially free is way easier than you ever thought of and in this book, you will come to know just

that. Just commit to being the person of the first kind and your life will never be the same again.

You were born great, you were born a winner, you were born a fighter. Proof of that is that you are alive and walking on your feet; you fought to walk, to talk, to run, to read, and a lot more. The reason you don't realize it is because you probably forgot it, or else you are wildly distracted. It's time to be laser-focused and not be distracted again, time to work on your financials and keep yourself and your family happy. Time to run in the right direction and be financially free now.

Let's get started.

In the first section of this book, we will be focusing on building a strong foundation, which is your real dreams, mindset, skill set, and toolset.

Without these four elements, you will always get stuck somewhere; you'll be very close to achieving your goals and all of sudden you'll lose it.

In the second section of this book, we will be talking about income generation—which is why you're here.

In the third section of this book, we will talk about how to scale and sustain your success and also keep it ever growing.

PS: In the end of the book there'll be some bonuses as well to keep you going.

SECTION 1:

FUEL YOUR ENGINE

CHAPTER 1

HAVE GUTS TO ACT ON YOUR DREAMS

A person without a dream is already dead and a dead person cannot achieve or change anything.

Dream . . . a small word to make the biggest changes in life, a small word to take you on the most adventurous journey of life, a small word to show you the possibilities of what you can have, a small word to show you what you can become, a small word to put your greatness and character in front of the world, a small word to your fortune and treasury . . . a small word which gives true meaning to your life, your existence.

So, live your dreams fearlessly because once you are dead, you won't be able to live them.

You have to, you should, and you must understand that your dreams are the foundation of your character, your outcomes, your fortunes, and your financial freedom. Small things make a huge difference in life and **huge differences produce massive results.**

Believing in your dreams and passions goes a long way on the path of success. This is not just the first step to financial freedom, it is also the entire ladder to success and you have to own this whole ladder and remember that the first step to financial freedom is your dream that you have not worked on yet.

To put it simply, your dreams are just like an ATM skull; your strategic action plan is the system which works internally and money is a reward of your efforts. To put it in layman's terms, this is your one-stop shop for all the ingredients of being successful financially. In talking about dreams, it can be said that **a dream is a cherished aspiration, ambition, or ideal.** A dream is what an individual works towards his entire life. Dreams may vary for different individuals that come from diverse backgrounds. This is because they have experienced different circumstances that make them into the person that they are. Hence, a dream is a culmination of all that you are as a person.

Be passionate about your dreams

There are many words that mean passion, namely hunger and thirst. These words show that just like food and water, passion is also a basic necessity that drives an individual on a day-to-day basis. This intense desire or enthusiasm for something is what makes one individual different from the rest. It is the defining factor of an individual.

Passion is the driving force of a dream; it makes dreams come alive, which is why you must be passionate about your dreams.

The first man on the moon—Neil Armstrong—would have never made it without all the individuals who were a part of the Apollo 11 mission. However, a name that is not much known—Buzz Aldrin—piloted the entire mission. This dream was a collective one, the success of which is attributed to NASA and all of America. Without the drive and dreams of each individual, even minutely part of the mission, this mission would not have been successful.

Imagine a mountaineer climbing up a mountain. Would he ever climb without defining the peak? Imagine a game of football, where players keep passing the ball to each other. There is no goal, so would they even think of scoring? What a monotonous game that would be! Now, imagine a game with two teams and two goal posts—just like a traditional game. Think of the energy and enthusiasm on the field. Players become competitive because of their goal to score. The audience cheer and shout, reflecting the enthusiasm of the field. Comparing this to real life, we can see that individuals are fired by their passions (means) towards their dream (end).

The dream of that footballer is not to score a goal but to become a good player or even the best player that ever existed on the planet. A goal is just a milestone towards your dreams. **Your goal is always smaller than your dreams**. This goes to show that **dreams can be seen, defined, and planned for**.

I went through a very rough patch in my childhood when my family faced bankruptcy for the first time. I would ask my parents for money but was always given 'no' as an answer. I understood it was not their fault as well. And as I walked to school each day just to save a few bucks, I'd think about the only thing that I wanted to change for my family: money.

I knew in those moments that I was weak and helpless, but I decided that I wouldn't remain this way my entire life and I asked myself: how can I be stronger and move through all the obstacles and how fast? This is where my dream of being rich was born. Hence, it is true that **dreams are built through circumstances and that passion is cultivated by the consequences and desperations faced during those circumstances**.

Although being rich was a dream that was formed very early on in my life, I had multiple other dreams that were conceived out of other circumstances. Every situation made me realize that I wanted to attain something more, something bigger than I did yesterday. With each dream I achieved, I got more and more inspired to attain my next dream. With every passion I pursued, I was stimulated to explore and implement more of my passions. This goes to show that **one individual can have multiple dreams and diverse passions in a lifetime.**

Although passions are the driving force to your dreams, it cannot be denied that dreams are different from passions. My dream was to become rich—this was my vision about my goal that was deep-seated in my brain. Dream was to be rich and passion was business.

A dream is an outcome and a passion is the way (action steps or activities towards outcomes).

However, my passion was earning through business. Thus, a passion is doing something that you love to do, again and again, with ease. It becomes easier when you practice it. There are many examples that show the difference between dreams and passion. A writer has a dream to publish a novel and sell a million copies. This is his dream. Supplementary to this, the actual art of writing—putting pen to paper—is his passion. This is something he loves doing. Another example is that of a fighter who wants to be titled as the best fighter; that is his dream and his passion is fighting.

When I slowly started attaining my dream of becoming rich, I realized another thing: as soon as I reach my goal, I have to aim higher and higher. I was not sure what my goal would be next. I did not know whether I was ready to move on from this dream yet. But, what I did know was that if I stopped at just one dream, I would not be passionate about anything and that would be as good as being dead.

The day you stop taking action on your dreams, the minute you get satisfied with what you have achieved, the second your dreams die, you die.

The positive side to this statement is that you can have any number of dreams and passions. Once I realized that, I kept forming goals in my head, and I kept working my way towards them slowly and steadily. I prioritized the dreams I wanted to achieve at that point in time. My decision was based on which dreams would take me where I needed to go. When I wanted to be rich, my dream of becoming a businessman would surely take me towards that end outcome. I chose my passion in a similar way. Working hard day in day out would fire me along my way to becoming rich.

Sometimes, in this quick-paced world, it becomes difficult to hold on to your dreams and passions. So, the question arises: how can one hold on to their dreams and passions? The answer is simple: **find strong emotional reasons to hold on**! Whether it is for yourself, your family, or your legacy, you simply have to find strongholds that will keep your dreams and passions in place. If you think of 'self', you should think about what you need in that moment of time and that will inspire you to pursue your dreams or passions. In thinking about family, think about what your family needs—money, support, growth—and that would be enough to keep you on the path to your dreams. When it comes to legacy, consider what you will be leaving behind, what will people say about you after you are no more. Each individual has his or her own reasons to hold on to their dreams or passions. The lesson here is simple—find strong reasons, and hold on!

The third time I faced bankruptcy, I lost a lot. I had no home, no place to sleep, even my girlfriend wasn't with me anymore. I had to sell my car, cell phone, and laptop. In short, I was left with nothing.

I asked myself then how much worse can it get? As a result of this, my dream was to become rich and I had strong reasons not to give up under any circumstances, and all my passions drove me towards my dreams. This is the story of many successful businessmen, and it is my story too. I believe that if something has been done before, it can be done again! If someone else with two hands and two legs has achieved it, I too can achieve it. There are successful businessmen in the world; you can be one too. All you need to do is believe. Believe in your dreams that it can be possible, believe that you can find the way to achieve them, believe that you have guts to take action and do whatever it takes. It is important to believe in yourself and break the belief system that has been established previously and is stopping you. I went against all odds and created my own path to become rich and successful. I fought the naysayers and my own inhibitions. I believed in simply one thing:

If it has been done once, it can be done again.

It comes only to those people who believe; magic happens when you believe in yourself and in your dreams. You shift your focus, focus creates flow of energy, flow of that energy creates emotions, emotions create behaviour, behaviour creates a questionnaire like how, when, what, why, who, where, and a lot more questions like that, and you start seeking answers, and when you seek answers, answers seek you with a blueprint. You start taking action and you start moving in the same direction and with every step, whether it is wrong or right, you get one step closer to your dreams.

A wrong decision towards your dream is always better than no decision.

The only thing that stops an individual from pursuing his or her dreams or passions is the fear of failure. However, the fear of failure never deterred me as a young boy because I was not motivated; my need was my motivation and when your need become your motivation you become functional and then you don't need to watch any motivational video.

I acted in spite of fear and learnt to control it so that I could chase my dreams and passions, and realize them gracefully. It can be said that as knowledge increases, fear decreases. As I got more and more knowledge about earning money, from reading books, listening to interview conversations, reading magazines, blogs, seminars, programs, and whatever I could get my hands on, apparently my permanent fear of failure decreased. This also goes to show that **no fear is permanent and every fear equals to one 'lack of a skill'.**

Dreams and passions are very important in life because they motivate and inspire an individual to reach their goal. In this process, a dream or passion drives an individual on a day-to-day basis. So, are you ready to break the belief system, follow your passion, and attain your dreams?

It is true that everybody has dreams. Deep down in your heart you strongly, desperately want to become something else but . . . that BUT is holding you; that BUT has put so many great people in the graveyard; that BUT is squeezing your heart, stabbing your back, killing your soul inside because you have hundred reasons not to act on them. Today, you must decide and commit to yourself that you won't die without fulfilling and living your own dreams. Today, you take an oath that you won't go into your grave without living the life of your dreams for one simple reason and the reason is: **you deserve to live your dreams.**

You must rescue yourself from the self-locked prison regardless of your situation and its presumed consequences.

In this moment, you will get out of this mess forever and nobody—I mean nobody—can pull you back ever again. There is only one person who can pull you back and that's you. I am going to give you the power of organized knowledge to keep you on the highest level you can think of, but first let's start with some amazing tips.

Here are some tips that will help you follow your dreams and pursue your passions only if you act. See, nothing will happen if you don't move at all. Nobody will help you, not even God himself. You have to understand that knowledge is useless unless you don't implement it in your life. Everything in this book is entirely based on my experience and I will share what I have done, what I do, or what would I do if I were you now. In the end of this chapter, I will share a blueprint with you that you can always review for reference to get unstuck in your pursuit of dreams or passions.

Here you go now!

1. **Have 10X Energy:** What I have realized is that even if you have dreams, are passionate, have a plan, and also know the way to success, sometimes you still won't take any action because you feel lazy to act and the reason behind that laziness is 'not enough energy'. I faced the same problem once but I recognized it immediately and designed my energy plan to address this situation. I started having high protein food: paneer, pulses, more water, fruits, dry fruits, juices, etc. I also started exercising on a daily basis, something I had left due to frequent travelling, and I was fired up in action.

You must see me when I am in action. It's like being in the clouds. People ask me whether I have taken drugs to generate that amount of energy . . . but I don't take drugs at all. Success, growth, and daily momentum work way better than drugs for me or for any other entrepreneur, I am sure. I prefer to smell money instead of drugs. You must have abundance of energy to create huge momentum, because there will be a lot of energy-sucking tasks, people, meetings and more throughout the day. Secondly, your energy level inspires others to work harder which is better for all entrepreneurs or future entrepreneurs. Thirdly, your energy levels control your body language and your tonality. When you have abundance of energy, you are going to feel good, look good, feel more confident, more powerful, and more in control.

The flip side, if it can be called that, of creating energy is that you have to be very conscious of how and where you are going to expend your focus and devote your time.

2. **Have your heart in it:** The second most important thing to help you get unstuck is to have your heart in it. If you don't want it with all of your heart, it simply means that the intensity of your dreams isn't very high and hence, you won't be passionate and you won't take action, no matter

how much knowledge you have. What I believe is that intensity of your emotions is the major driving force behind your dreams. You have to put your best foot forward and chase after your dreams by putting your emotions into it. Good news is that if you are serious but your intensity is low then you can connect or plug your emotions to your dreams to create momentum. You *can* find emotional dots. Remember if you can put your heart into something, your approach will change, and as soon as your approach changes, results will be different and sometimes beyond your imagination. An example of this is that if you're working for a company, imagine it to be yours. Each good day is beneficial to you and hence you will start putting your entire energy into making it successful. Regardless of your location, job designation, and any other factors, if you start treating your job as your own business, or a borrowed car from your friend as your own, just ask yourself what will change in your behaviour, and what will change in results? A small shift in perspective will create a huge impact for your own good.

3. **Define your ACTION MANTRA:** Defining your action mantra will keep you going, it will make you do things that are needed and not just what you want in that moment. It will make you

an unstoppable force like the Hulk. Whatever mantra makes you jump into action, define it. Say it to yourself over and over till it gets ingrained into your brain. Whether it is working twelve hours a day, or just two hours, make sure that each moment you spend is worthwhile. Remember, time is life—if you don't catch up now, you never will. I will tell you what my action mantra is. Three simple words: whatever it takes.

Yes, once I decide to do something then I am prepared to do whatever it takes to achieve it, and no hurdles, obstacles, problems, negative people or any other force can stop me from getting there. I don't care about hardships, and neither should you.

4. **Don't forget about your rescue door:** A rescue door is something which can get you out of the unbreakable jail, you just need to keep asking the question 'how' until you get the answer. You might be in financial prison—or a toxic relationship, which is more like prison itself. Whether you want a solution to your financial crisis or you simply want to start a new relationship or a new business, the question *how* will give you all the answers. Use this rescue door whenever you feel stuck. This is the one thing that will set you apart from everybody else. Think of it, you are reading this book because it will answer your hows.

5. **Follow the footprints:** Alternative ways to start working on your dreams are super easy. If you want to free yourself and have a clear path to success then look at other successful people in the same domain and industry, and follow their footprints because success always leaves footprints. Find out how was their journey to success, what did they study, where did the study, what experience did they gain, what sort of mindset do they have, etc. Or if you have a role model who has taken certain steps to success and you are aware of it, then ensure that you follow their footprints. Make your own decisions, but use their plan as the basis for these decisions. Finding successful footprints is very easy today—you can make a list of names of those people and read their biographies, watch their interviews, read the top ten or twenty books on each skill they have or those that you require in order to become successful. Content is the prime source of any skill and it can be divided into four categories: text, videos, images, and audio. Tap into all four and fortify yourself with knowledge.

6. **Lack of a skill equals fear:** When I was stuck and I asked myself why and what I was afraid of, I started writing my answers in my hotel room, and I realized that there was a fear inside me and the fear was there because I didn't have that particular skill. Next, I asked myself if my fear

would disappear if I acquired that skill? And the answer was a big yes.

This blueprint, which I will be sharing with you in the end of this chapter, was created that time. Always remember that if there is fear then a skill is lacking; find out that skill you need to acquire and gain as much knowledge as you can related to your skill. Once you have all the knowledge, you will be a master of that skill. And once you have the skill, you won't fear trying and failing anymore. An example for this is that suppose you want to become a speaker but have never spoken on the stage. So, you will have some fear of speaking in front of an audience. But, if you take a course on how to become a public speaker and master this skill within months or a year, then you won't be ever afraid. Being fearful because of the paucity of a skill is what you have to overcome.

7. **Know thyself:** The most important thing is to know yourself. Understand what it is that you truly want. Recognize the patterns of your life. Know your mission, vision, know your potential, know your weaknesses and work on them. Know your strong points and cash on them and take action daily. Make a daily, weekly, monthly, and yearly plan. These sound like fairly simple steps, but this is what will set you apart from the rest. You know, 98% of the people don't really know themselves.

Do what the 2% does, or do completely opposite of what the majority does—know thyself.

8. **Be the second fastest:** It doesn't matter if you started something second or third or even at the hundredth number, what matters is how fast you move. Yahoo was first but Google was the second fastest; Friendster was first but Facebook was the second fastest; IBM was first but Apple was the second fastest. The best news for you is that you can be the second fastest anytime during your journey. The second benefit of starting in the second place is that you learn a lot from others' mistakes—and success as well—so you can do better. **Speed is what matters most in order to become successful in life**. Whatever your dreams are, just have a strategic plan ready, and implement it with the speed of a rocket.

9. **Remember that you were born a winner:** Yes! That's right. You were born successful because you won out of million sperms. You also have been falling since childhood, but it doesn't matter because your approach was different. You couldn't walk in your first few attempts; you couldn't run once you started walking. You couldn't read in the first few days; you couldn't read words in the first few attempts. **Trying and not succeeding is not failure. The reason you are able to walk and run now is that you kept at it and kept**

improving your weak areas. Most importantly, you did it for the joy of doing, unknowingly, because your mind was not loaded with dirt. Now you know that you were a born winner so what you can do knowingly is that you can start doing things for the joy of doing, like a child does.

10. **Compare outcomes:** I never believe what I hear until I don't measure it from all possible angles, and now, I don't even need to do that because my brain operates on the top level, which is the functional level, and I don't seek motivation. You must know what dreams are worth fighting for and what can hurt you or paralyse you in life, and keeping this in mind, you must act accordingly. Ask yourself what will you lose and gain? If you lose more than you can gain and losing can be beyond recovery then don't do it. But if you gain more than you can lose then you must do it now. In real life, things work differently than motivational talks and 'be positive' lectures. You can act upon what looks right and profitable but saving yourself from unrepairable loss is the biggest challenge. Now compare and add the precious experience you are going to earn to your gaining list and act accordingly.

11. **Failing is a sign of progress:** It is important to fail because that makes you realize that at least you are doing something. The fact here is that the

one who takes action, will definitely be in a better position than the one who doesn't take any action. Wrong action is better than inaction, and failing is hence a sign of mental progress if nothing else. If you fail once and get back up, you will find new ways to solve the problems. When I teach sales or marketing in my own organization, I ask them to try to fail, get rejected, get used to NO because it will come later whether you want it or not. But, **if you can handle rejections, NOs, and failures easily in the first place then it will never matter later. If your mind can process that information that setbacks don't matter at all, then in the process you become unstoppable.** Secondly, failures will make you frustrated to a level and that's where you put more pressure on your brain to seek another solution, and a lot more psychological activities towards the journey of your success.

12. **A setback is a set up for comeback:** Any problems that you face, any hurdles that you encounter, rejections you receive, or bankruptcy you go through are all setting you up for your comeback. If life and your circumstances have knocked you down, it doesn't mean you are going to stay there. If people have betrayed you, cheated you financially, and you are left with nothing, it doesn't mean you won't get up, that you won't fight back!

This phase . . . this pain is temporary. So, get back up and fight for your honour and pride because you deserve to live your dreams. Life knocked me down so many times but I never accepted my defeat. I faced bankruptcy and had to leave the city of my dreams, Mumbai, but I realized this setback was actually a set up to make me rich and successful. Twelve months later, I came back and became a millionaire. Decide to bounce back, decide to come back as a tight slap to the naysayers, with your unreachable status and massive success.

13. **Be energetic:** Unless you are fired up, have enthusiasm, and are passionate, nothing will be possible. Make sure that you are energetic whenever you are working. It is okay to take breaks, but come back refreshed and ready to take off.

Be serious in life and let your dreams come alive, grow through what you deserve and touch others' lives. Below is the exact blueprint that I have used to stay unstuck and free. It is simple, but super powerful, and you'll know its power only when you write it down and implement it.

Follow my magical blueprint to get unstuck on your dreams, in your life.

#1. What's your real dream? What dreams you have been holding on to?

(If you die in the next five minutes what would you regret most not doing?)

1._____
2._____
3._____
4._____
5._____

#2. Why are you holding back? Write down your fears, reasons, excuses, etc.

1._____
2._____
3._____
4._____
5._____

#3. What do you need to do in order to pursue your dreams? What skills do you need to learn against each reason/excuse/fear?

1._____
2._____
3._____
4._____
5._____

#4. Which institutes, gurus, or people can help you the most? Who has helped your role model? Write about highest quality sources.

1._____

2._____

3._____

4._____

5._____

CHAPTER 2

ACQUIRE A
FINANCIAL MINDSET

Mindset is the established set of habits or attitudes held by someone towards their dreams or passions. In simple terms, mindset can be defined by your actions and reactions—it is about how you entertain the world and how you engage in activities. Your mindset is the key to success because it promotes the underlying belief that you control your own destiny.

Success comes to your mind first, later in reality.

Any great success has been acquired in the mind first, any war has been won in the mind of the winner first. Any championship has been won in the mind of the player first. This is why it is very important to have a positive mindset with a high-quality processor. Yes, your mind is just like a processor. Think about it like this:

Mindset = Mind + Set

This means to set your mind on a frequency

to attain success. This is known as altitude of attitude, which equals to your success in reality world.

Frequency → Thoughts → Emotions → Behaviour → Habits → Attitude→ Altitude of Attitude equals Success.

The right attitude attracts success. This is the key outcome of a right mindset.

Mindset works in day-to-day life as well as in a long-term perspective. This set of habits or attitudes drastically changes the way you look at both life and your dreams. In the positive realm, a growth mindset is one where an individual looks at growing each and every day. Being in such a mindset, people believe that their most basic abilities can be developed through hard work and dedication.

A great mindset is about distributing its physical, mental, emotional, and spiritual energy on self-vision or planned outcomes. There are ground rules to obtain desired results through your actions. A great mindset allows you to make the right decisions, have a right plan and the right implementation at the right time. A right mindset is entirely focused on outcomes and encourages you to do what is required or needed to achieve success or follow your dreams. Basically, how successful you are going to be depends on your mindset, the altitude of your attitude. If you want to be rich, then you must have a rich mindset. If you want to be wealthy, then you must have a wealthy mindset. If you want to be financially free, then you must have a financially free mindset. Now, the billion dollar question is: how to develop a mindset.

Q1. Why will you change your mindset?

_____

_____

Q2. What are your goals?

_____

_____

Q3. What will be the connector between your mindset and your goals? Reason for reaching there? Reasons for not giving up under any circumstances?

_____

_____

_____

Q4. What will be the quality of the content you are going to feed your mind with?

_____

_____

_____

Q5. Where are you going to find such content?

_____

_____

_____

Q6. What will be the source of that knowledge/content?

_____

_____

_____

Videos, Audios, Text, Images

There are multiple types of content, including different mediums and the ways in which they can be used. Use your eyes as a medium for visual content in the form of videos, TV shows, and plays. Use your ears as a medium for auditory content in the form of music, audio books, seminars, webinars, and podcasts. Use text in terms of books, blogs, websites, and slideshows. Use images in terms of pictures, imagination, and visualization.

How can you use content to develop your mindset?

1. Find most successful speakers, authorities on the topic of your choosing.
2. Find out videos, seminars, and webinars and watch them for forty to sixty minutes per week.
3. Find relevant podcasts, audio books from the top ten authorities.
4. Read the top ten books on the relevant topic—read two books a week. The rationale is that for every skill you want, read ten books.

A habit is a settled or regular tendency or practice, especially one that is hard to give up. It is a fact that you cannot unlearn a habit. But the good news is that you can replace it with another habit by practicing better. I had so many problems with handling cash. Even after earning a large amount each month, I went bankrupt multiple times. Spending on useless things had become a habit for me. Then one day, I decided to change my habits and began learning about saving and investment. I replaced the habit of spending with the habit of investing and saving by practicing better habits.

Within the growth mindset, there are multiple sub-parts:

1. **Responsibility**—It is not only taking up responsibility. Do not plan it if you cannot implement it. Take responsibility only if you are able to respond to your responsibility. This is the only way you can fulfil it. Being responsible is equivalent to being able to respond, and that is the ultimate way of fulfilling your responsibilities.

2. **Commitment**—Commitment is an oath to your goals and to yourself. It is a promise to yourself. When you decide to do something, a definite decision that you will not give up, no matter what happens should be in place. Whether it is negative or positive, you will stay committed in life towards your dreams or goals.

3. **Discipline**—Being punctual and dedicated towards the fact that you are going to do something on a regular basis. Even if you are tired and feel like giving up, you still do the task at hand because you are disciplined. Discipline is doing what is needed and not what you want. It is not

what you should, but what you must. It is about being functional with or without motivation.

4. **Focus**—Doing one thing at one time is called being focused. Think about a horse race—the horses are given blinders to focus on the track. In life, this means narrowing down your options. Even the biggest things will look small if you focus. Linked to this, you must have a new definition of multi-tasking: doing many things in a day, but only one thing at one time.

5. **Routine**—Routine is a plan-ahead program—doing things at a time that was decided by you so that you can achieve the results that you want. Routine takes time to give results, it is subject to being followed for a period of time. The thing that makes a routine successful is time. It is a waste of time if you do not do it at the given time. Routine is about doing your things first in the first place and not entertaining any other objects.

6. **Set goals**—If you do not have a goal, you will have nowhere to go. Goals give you a direction or path to follow. Your goals will be your destination and an outcome, which will be highly beneficial today or in the long run.

7. **Plan to Implement**—People work on the wrong plans. They have a misconception that it is the right plan—like the fact that the sun 'rises' is wrong; the earth simply spins on its axis is another

misconception. Similarly work on the plan that is correct. Running in the wrong direction will never let you win the race. There are some steps to follow for planning to implement:

a. Never work on the wrong plan.

b. R & D: Spend more time on planning. You can do this by reading books or listening to speeches of your role models. R & D helps to make a perfect plan.

c. Now plan: Find out the right aspects of the plan to work on. Based on the 20-80 rule, find what 20% of work will give you 80% results. For a salesman, the plan will look something like this:

Date: / /   Sales Productivity Planner   Target/Potential:

#1. Closing Today . . .	#2. Follow Ups Today . . .
1.	1.
2.	2.
3.	3.
4.	4.
5.	5.
#3. Pitching Today . . .	**#4. Maintaining Relationship with . . .**
1.	1.
2.	2.
3.	3.
4.	4.
5.	5.
#5. Self-Development . . .	**#Notes/Reminders/To-Do List . . .**
Time:	1.
Action:	2.
....	3.
Time:	4.
Action:	5.

- Closing Today—Nothing happens until something is sold in a company or as an individual.
- Follow-ups—People who will pay you soon, people you have met and invested your time and energy with, need to be followed up with.
- Pitching Today—New clients who will be talking to you, meeting you, and will be paying you tomorrow.

- Maintaining Relationships—These are the people who have bought from you and are now your clients or people you have met but haven't converted into clients as yet. You have something valuable to share with them on a regular basis over mails or over a meeting once in a while.

- Self-Development—Upgrade your sales skills using all types of content, decide what new things you are going to learn today, what strategies, what lessons, etc.

  There is no point of planning if you are not going to implement it. Planning can give you temporary satisfaction but implementation is a permanent solution and a must.

8. **Take action**—The world is a brutal battleground. Even if you want to survive or win the game, you need to fight—fight for your dreams, fight for your family, fight for your rights, fight for your success . . . fight for the life you deserve. Thus, taking action is fighting for yourself. Despite knowing the fact that you might fail, you might be afraid, it's risky, you might lose, you might get beaten in the ring, you *still* go into the ring. Because if you fight, there are equal chances of you winning as the other person who has experience. But if you do not fight, defeat is guaranteed. So, take action—be the man of action and you will be favoured by God.

9. **Control your mind**—Doing what is needed is a part of controlling your mind. You should control your mind; your mind should not control you. When you lose control over your mind, you are not focusing on your business. You have to be aware of your thoughts and the outcomes. If you can watch your thoughts, you can control them.

When your mind tells you to do something, you have to ask consciously:
1. Why?
2. What will the result be?
3. Will it be in my favour?
If it is not in your favour, back off.
Developing growth mindset can be achieved in the following ways:
1. Immerse yourself in quality content.
2. Stop justifying everything.
3. Engage yourself with work all the time.
4. Don't be so hard on yourself.
5. Don't praise anybody on your expense.
6. Be experimental, try everything.
7. Do things for the joy of doing.
8. Stop looking out for free things, that's an emotional debt.
9. Don't try to be perfect.
10. Do first things first as planned.
11. Decide to be a man/woman of action.
12. Seek your life alone.

13. Don't seek for permissions or approvals.
14. Be clear about what you want and how you want something.
15. Be consistent.
16. Destroy all your distractions.
17. Stop caring about negative people.
18. Love yourself first.
19. Give before you ask.
20. Stop complaining.
21. Be an executor, not an excuser.
22. Stop being afraid of rejections or failures forever.
23. Wake up early, shine before the sun.
24. Listen to motivational audios/videos in the first thirty minutes you wake up.
25. Do what is needed, not what you want.
26. Workout daily.
27. Stop trying to please everybody else.
28. Don't take what is not yours rightfully.
29. Leave things better than you found them.
30. Read books every single day.
31. Find the purpose of your living.
32. Start living in the present instead of past or future, but work for the future.
33. Whatever you do, do it with best of your abilities to be great, not average.
34. Don't rape your dreams.
35. Take that first baby step which will make you a man of honour.

Chapter 3

CHAPTER 3

AVOID THE TRAP OF MULTIPLE STREAMS OF INCOME

Wrong advices or decisions can spoil your life. The most stupid thing people are told is that of creating multiple streams of income, but that's entirely stupid because if you try to create an additional source of income without having a necessary skill, then you will fall and fail miserably. Income is an outcome of a skill, so it's better if you have multiple streams of skills instead of multiple streams of income. Income without skill won't sustain for a long period of time but if you master multiple skills, your income will flow for generations and you will be making money even after you are dead. Google how MJ is still making money, how Napoleon Hill is still bringing in riches! Actually, they aren't just making money, they are printing money.

The Art of Acquiring Multiple Skills

Moving forward from fulfilling your dreams, and developing a success-oriented mindset, skills are the primary reason for the success or failure of an individual. If you are skilled in the right direction towards your dream or passion, you are most likely to succeed.

However, **fear of failure is born from the lack of such skills**.

In this chapter we will talk about acquiring multiple skills because multiple streams of skills will create multiple streams of income—passive income for the rest of your life or maybe for generations to come—and it's easier nowadays than ever.

Once an individual acquires the necessary skill, the fear of failure reduces and one is more likely to succeed. There are many examples that prove this point. Before you learnt driving, were you not fearful of accidents? Once an individual learns how to drive a car, this skill helps in reducing the fear of an accident, i.e., the fear of failure. Similarly, were you not afraid of the water before you learnt how to swim? Were you not afraid of falling before you learnt how to ride a horse? Were you not afraid of approaching the person you had a crush on?

After acquiring the necessary skills, the fear of failure will reduce or be removed because you now have increased knowledge about the task. This is how it works: **skills build strong knowledge, and knowledge builds confidence, confidence turns into action, action produces results, and results give you an unforgettable experience of comfort, luxury, happiness, growth, success, and a feeling of fulfilment, and that changes everything in your life.** Imagine learning how to ride a bike. Acquiring the necessary skills builds strong knowledge about riding, which builds your confidence to ride a bike. Now that you have confidence, you are more likely to ride the bike freely (action), which produces results. You can even become a bike-racer if you want to!

As an example of skills acquisition, I want to share a short story with you: I had a huge fight with five guys when I was in the seventh grade. I wasn't the strongest kid around, back then, and got beaten up because of my lack of strength. For the next three days my body felt battered. I was in pain and felt constantly tired. But I wanted to change that. So, when an opportunity to learn karate came my way, I took it. Since then, I have learnt martial arts from different places and fought in national championships. Physically I became stronger, faster than ever. Suddenly, my fear disappeared—what I realized was that I worked on my dream to become a stronger man and during the process of learning martial arts I enjoyed it a lot. But I also practiced a lot, which gave me high intensity confidence to defend myself against anybody and the fear disappeared forever.

There are some facts related to skills that must be discussed in order to understand skill acquisition. The primary and most important fact is that **any skill can be acquired.** Think of a little boy who likes playing football. If he practices and learns all the rules about football, he can possibly become a successful football player. Imagine that you have a dream to become a motivational speaker. By following your dreams, you can develop your mindset in the ways mentioned above and learn the skills of conversation, presentation, and body language that are needed for you to become a successful motivational speaker.

The next fact is that **behind each and every fear there is a skill that is lacking.** The same individual who wants to become a motivational speaker might have stage fright that stems from lack of knowledge. Once he gains the skill of public speaking and gets more knowledgeable, this fear will definitely reduce. Another thing is that fear can also arise from having partial skills. If the footballer only learns how to play in one position on the field (defender), he will feel less skilled than those who can play in any position. He must therefore gain complete knowledge and experience about football in order to eliminate any fear related to playing the game. Thus, behind every fear there is a lack of skills or a half-worked skill.

Fact number three is that a **skill is a process of learning something new, which requires a fixed amount of time, energy, and effort on a daily basis.** Many actors, before reaching the pinnacle of success, give themselves years to practice the various aspects of acting. Before John Terry drew a cheque of ten million, he gave himself three long years where he worked on himself rather than looking for external success. To attain long-term success that sustains, it is essential to understand that one must practice their skill on a daily basis for a fixed amount of time, putting in the energy and effort. For a writer to become successful, he has to practice his skills each and every day.

A start-up, for example, has various aspects that need to be up and running before the business can be launched. Many start-up entrepreneurs take years to gain and practice the essential skills of marketing, finance, human resource, etc. Imagine if you wanted to open a bakery, you would first have to learn baking to ensure that your bakers were doing their jobs perfectly. Then you would have to understand from where to purchase your raw materials and in what quantity. You would also have to learn marketing to promote your business and human resources to hire employees. These are just some examples of skills that require practice and dedication to ensure that your company runs smoothly. Thus, a **skill requires practice every day—not just physical, but mental, emotional, financial, and spiritual.**

If you want to learn yoga, you have to wake up every day at a given time, put in the effort and energy to learn the asana perfectly to ensure that you don't harm your body. Yoga is an art and learning the skill of meditation requires dedication and practice each and every day. This is not just to say that you have to physically practice the asana but to also mentally prepare yourself for an hour or more of quiet meditation. It also requires you to be emotionally strong and financially and spiritually independent. Imagine that you are now skilled in the art of yoga; you still have to wake up at the same time and practice this skill to make it a part of your everyday routine.

A cricketer, to become successful, has to work on stamina, strength, flexibility, speed, focus, movements, diet, and net practice. He can't depend on only one skill to become the best cricket player possible. MS Dhoni had to be an all-rounder to gain the name and success that he has gained today. Thus, **one skill alone can't help you become successful.** Every skill has its own tail or family of skills. Think back to the motivational speaker. He learns multiple skills from the same family of skills to reach the pinnacle of success. He has to become an effective speaker and hence, has to learn related skills of speaking, body language, gestures, etc. Speaking is just the primary skill; the supplementary skills are—leadership, art of habit formation, breaking belief systems, building confidence, creating content, presentation skills, relative vocabulary, diction, tonality, modulation, gestures, expression, and body language. These skills together are what make a speaker effective and successful.

When NASA launched its first trip to the moon, everything had to work in order to prevent a crash. Similarly, for an individual to be successful, he must work on more than just one skill—he must work on a family of skills that will ensure that he becomes successful. Another example of this is that an actor works on observation, imagination, visualization, communication, emotions, development of feelings, building character, meditation, fight moves, dance, and body language. There is a lot more that he has to gain in order to become a successful actor, but once he gains the entire family of skills there is nothing that can stop him from becoming a blockbuster actor.

A hockey team designs and practices certain moves over a thousand times. In this way, all the players become accustomed to the moves and during the game, they know exactly what to do. Thus, to become successful, **find your best moves and practice three thousand times.** Obama, to become a successful and liked president of the United States, must have practiced his speeches at least a couple of times to make sure that he impacted the audience in the best way possible. If someone like Obama can do it, why can't you? The most successful individuals know that practicing their best moves develops them and also helps them in obtaining new skills. In practicing his speech, Obama becomes dedicated to this daily practice. He hence acquired the skill of dedication.

A half-learned skill can be harmful just like half-baked knowledge is harmful. Perfection means you keep working and stay up-to-date with your skill. A coder who doesn't learn the most popular coding language will be wasting his skill by just sticking to what he knows. He must move with the times and understand the more time you spend on working on your skill, the more skilled you become. So, **practice to perfection.** Remember, whatever you were yesterday, you are more today. And whatever you are today, you will be better tomorrow. So, take up your skills, follow these steps, and you will be on the path to success.

START YOUR JOURNEY

CHAPTER 4

A PLAN
FOR INCOME

Once you have established your dreams and passions, developed your mindset and acquired the necessary skill set, the next step is to plan for income. What is important is that you focus on your dreams, mindset, and skill towards making the maximum income that you can earn and finding people who will be ready to pay you for what you have learnt. The first question you need to answer is:

Who needs your skills most? Who you can help most? Who can gain maximum benefits?

_____

_____

_____

To answer this question, you should understand the importance of your skill and the implementation of the same.

If you are passionate to become a singer, your singing skills will be required as a playback singer, lead vocalist, on singing shows, etc. Now that you know where your skill is needed, decide who needs it the most.

This means that if someone is desperately seeking for a playback singer, that person needs your skill more than the producer of a singing show that has millions of applicants. Hence, you should go for the opportunity that requires your skill and will appreciate the talents once you join them as an employee or as a partner.

The second question you need to ask is: **Who can pay you the most for utilizing your skills?**

_____

_____

_____

Imagine you are a marketer and you have identified that there are hundred business categories that require your skills in equal desperation. According to me, you should serve the market that can pay you well. You must remember that you shouldn't work with people who have money but are not willing to pay, and you should also never work with people who have a will to pay but have no money. If you serve those two market segments then you will work hard throughout your life and can never be financially free.

Once you have determined who needs your skills the most and who can pay you the most for utilizing your skills, the next step is to **make a list** of such companies. I personally believe that planning is the most important step in any decision-making process. So, make a list of all the companies that fit the above-mentioned criteria.

Make sure that you pick only the top companies in the field that your skill set lies in. Always narrow down your audience and be laser focused.

Next, **prepare your pitch** as a company or as an employee. Your pitch is defined by how you present yourself. Right from the first email you send out to your interviewer, everything about your pitch must be impeccably planned. Prepare your resume to stand out and ensure that you add all your work experience. In your interview/conversation/interaction, be confident, passionate, and positive. People will hire you if you present yourself to be profitable for them. Think, would you hire yourself if you were the owner of the company? If not, change your pitch and change it again, until you think you would hire yourself.

Once you are perfectly prepared, **approach** the short-listed companies. This is a simple step as you send in your CVs, schedule interviews, etc. The next step is: **convert**. Learn to give before you expect to get. Conversion is an art and begins with finding loopholes, areas of improvement in the company you are looking to get hired in. These are the things that they are not doing that will help them grow as a company. Tell them what and how they can improve on such points without asking for a job. There is an MBA college in Delhi NCR. A friend of mine graduated from there and was looking for a job. He asked me for help and I gave him the same idea of conversion.

This guy was from IT; he researched properly and

went to the interviewed prepared. Once they seated him, and asked some questions, he, after some time, told them that they had so many loopholes and that he was going to talk about a few, and tell them what they could do to sort it out. He opened their website, showed them an issue and told them how someone could delete their data and make a loss of a huge amount and also jeopardize their hard-earned reputation in a minute. He then went on and told them what they should do to fix it.

Not surprisingly, he was hired in half an hour without any second or third round of interviews. This is the true art of conversion, which led him to get the job. Why? You must never forget that people will buy to avoid problems than finding solutions in life or business. That interview was closed to avoid problems that could have done irreplaceable damage. One additional tip I would like to share with you is that if you looking for a job and not getting it, then you have to break in. What I mean is that you just find an internship or do some volunteer work in your dream companies or in companies who will pay you the most.

Focus on Income:

Once you are clear about your income then start focusing on it. That's not easy at all. People have this tendency to spread their focus on random activities or unplanned activities. You need to think a lot . . . a lot . . . throughout the day about generating income. No less than ninety per cent of your time should be dedicated towards the ideology of how can you generate more income.

Chapter 5

CREATE EVERLASTING STREAMS AND SOURCES OF INCOME

Money is not a game of investments, saving, or spending; it's a game of earning. Savings or spending don't make anybody rich and neither do investments, it's your abilities and approach to earn money out of savings, spending, and investments that makes you rich. You must understand that saving, spending, and investment is a part of earning and its distribution. Return on investment is also a part of your earning abilities; same goes for saving and spending.

You must spend your maximum time thinking about earnings from multiple sources.

There are three main powerful reasons and qualities to get rich in life and to sustain that status: ability, capability, and disability.

Ability to earn more and more money is simply great and a skill few people can maintain but this can result in two things: riches and poverty. This might sound a little odd but let me explain. If you are capable of controlling your financial outcomes then you will reap riches, but if you are disabled in utilizing existing earning or amount, then it will be all spent, and soon you will be left with nothing but poverty.

Capability is about controlling your financial outcomes out of investments, budgeting, distributing, spending, savings, etc. Capability is a sign that you will be filthy rich in life.

Disability of utilizing existing funds results in poverty for sure. To mismanage your life or financials, you don't have to do anything except spending all you get. But getting rich needs serious planning and execution on time.

What I am going to disclose in this book, I wish I knew when I started out, or even a bit later. I tried to listen to so many financial gurus but on practical ground, nothing worked, because they all were just a talk show, misleading innocent people on purpose to earn their own fortunes. What I realized was that they all focused on investing, but did not guide people on where to invest, how to invest, the other DOs and DON'Ts, strategies, etc. and while a few of them talked about the importance of earning, they never walked anybody step-by-step on how to increase their earnings and incomes. Why should they have done this? Because when you buy in, you have some expectations, some hopes, and if your hopes are not fulfilled, it's harmful to your emotional as well as spiritual health. As a result, most of us stop trying, stop trusting, start overthinking, and all these are poisonous to our wealth and the fortunes we would have made or we might be missing on now for the same reasons. These so-called gurus will talk about the finest steps but not about the foundational traits. A true mentor never hides the most precious knowledge from his students. In this chapter we will talk about increasing your income and filling your income account, so let's get started on generating some income for you . . .

Don't try to just read and pass the information, let it sink in. Read again and again if you don't understand in one shot.

#1. Increase your earning skills deeper

Every individual, business owner, and investor has a different level of ability to generate income. However, your ability to earn with the same skills is higher if you think about the options. In order to do this, you **increase your earning skills deeper, or vertically.** This can be done by acquiring more and more operative active knowledge on the same topic. Read more books, study trends, join mentorship programs, and attend seminars. Find more sources of acquisition: online courses, volunteer work, and internships. A sales person for example can learn more sales tactics and crack more deals to produce more results. A business owner can learn more about business strategies, people management, time management, and revenue management. An investor can learn about investments, funding, etc.

A simple example of increasing skills deeper is the iPhone series that developed the phones in the same category, from iPhone 4 – 5 – 6 – 7 – 8 and later iPhone X and so on. This can also be termed as upgrading yourself. The Apple brand explored the options for growth and did not bind itself by any limitations. Sometimes, people feel like they do not want to go higher than their potential. But they don't know that their potential is always higher than their targets. Think about it like this: a tree grows above the ground as well as below. The more the tree grows below the ground, the more it will grow above. So, keep upgrading yourself and learn how to grow your earning skills deeper by acquiring new valuable knowledge.

#2. Increase your earning skills wider

Once you believe that you are well merged with growing deeper and you manage your time well, it is time to **create room to grow wider.** This means adding additional skills to your profile as an employee, business owner, or investor. Based on your interests and dreams, pick a skill and master it. It is important to remember that an additional skill will never make you weaker. By default, every person has at least ten skills to work on. By the age of sixteen or eighteen or twenty, you have all these skills and interest built in. Figuring out what these skills are is difficult. Polishing the skills is even more difficult. But, earning more from these skills is a task and responsibility of a lifetime.

Additional skills can be added to create additional sources of income. When you realize during a market crash or some other situation that going deeper in one specific subject or niche is harmful, diversification is the answer.

"Diversify your skills instead of your income."

How do I diversify my skills?

I learn a new skill every third or sixth month, depending on what skill I am acquiring. But if you have only one skill like I had long back, then you are in trouble for sure. Think about a stockbroker or trader who faces a serious market crash or think about a real estate agent who faces a fall in the real estate industry. What is he going to do with his time when he realizes that he has no other skill and he cannot function in the specific industry that he does have skills in? A perfect example of diversification of skills is Priyanka Chopra. She started out as a model, became Miss World then went into acting and then diversified into singing and then into acting in the west, and is now a world-famous celebrity. What is a teacher going to do when there are no jobs in the teaching industry? The answer is: grow wider! Think about the Apple watch, the iPad, the iPod, the iPhone, MacBook laptops, Apple TV—this is a clear example of growing wider. Do not bind yourself with one skill, that's a dead end.

Fortunes are made with deeper and wider growth; it is mandatory to have additional primary and secondary skill sets. Remember the lessons from chapter 3? You can look at any wealthy person and try to find out what he or she does. Eventually you will find out that they have multiple sources of income and the reason behind having multiple sources of income is that they have additional primary skills and secondary skill sets.

#3. Income distribution and management

If you have decided to grow your skills deeper and wider just like the Apple brand or any other investor or a celebrity, you are now prepared to think about income. Primarily, the distribution and management of income. The big question is:

How do you manage money?

Earning money is not a very difficult task as it may seem but what is more difficult is how people manage it. Management of money plays a very critical role in the life of a wealthy, middle class or poor person.

Usually when a layman gets income, they spend it on shopping, eating, drinking, paying bills, and buying other things. This is a cancer that must be removed if you want to be rich or wealthy and take charge of your life for yourself and your family. On the other hand, when a rich person gets his income, he distributes this money. This shows that if you do not know how to manage or distribute your money, you will go down the hill very fast without breaks. There is no alternative route to being successful. Think about a movie trailer. For example, there is a bad movie but its trailer is distributed well. This movie will do better than a good movie that does not distribute its trailer well. I am sure you must have seen movies that are hundred times better than ones who made 10x, 50x or 100x money.

#4. Income Distribution

There are four different accounts in which you can distribute your money from your income account or salaried account right when you get the income and this is what I do; this is what has set me up in life.

Investment: In this account you wire a big chunk of your monthly income to cash out on investment opportunities to generate income without much effort and involvement.

Current: In this account you wire a medium chunk of your monthly income to manage day-to-day business operations, to cover fixed expenses like office or home rent, credit card bills, EMIs, electricity bills, telephone bills, etc.

Saving: In this account you wire a small chunk of your monthly income to help some specific people, treat yourself well, buy some luxury items for yourself which make you feel good, hobbies, learning activities and earn some active incentives in value inflation by buying gold, silver, copper, etc.

Emergency: Life is unpredictable, anything can happen. We shouldn't think or focus on bad events, which *might* occur but we should be prepared for any eventuality.

Just like there are four accounts, there are also four levels of distribution. When you are starting out, you can follow exactly what I did, but I used to increase the percentage in between:

1st Year: 20:10:60:10, deposit 20% in investment account, 10% in saving account, 60% in current account as you might have huge expenses, 10% emergency account.

2nd Year: 40:10:30:20

3rd Year: 50:15:20:15

Once you start following this you can adjust and change the percentage, spend openly, save more, but focus on earning more than anything else. Just think about creating income sources and generating more money. Soon, within three to six months, if you take 20% or 30%

out of your income, it will be equal to your 60% expenses. That's an awesome feeling, an exclusive feeling, which will be experienced by those who are ready to implement this plan with the speed of a lion. You can also download this plan from my website.

#5. Debt Distribution

Debt is not an income even though you make money out of it; income will be the profit or positive cash flow created or generated from the debt you received. However, if it is debt amount (loan), then you must be ready with an investment plan before you get it and invest 100%. One ground rule is that you should never pay debt with debt. The second rule is that do not put debt into inactive activities which can't generate higher income than the interest rate you are paying to the bank or any NBFCs or others. This will put you in a downward spiral that nobody can save you from, and soon you will have to sell lot of things to pay it back to the lenders. Your debt has to be invested, protected, and multiplied over the period.

#6. Types of Income

I was not a money guy so I broke it in a simple manner for my better understanding. There are four distinct sources of income that must be discussed for you to be able to manage and distribute your income—

A. Investment Income
B. Earned Income
C. Passive Income
D. Portfolio Income

Let's try to understand this.

A. Investment Income: Investment Income is divided in two major parts:

- **Active Investment**—This is all the money that you receive once a month or once a year. Active investment makes you money month by month, every month. An example of this is if you lend Rs. 1000000 at 3% interest rate per month then every month you will receive Rs. 30000/- as an active income. Another example of this is if you rent a flat @ Rs. 50,000 and then rent it out on a higher rate of 20% extra which comes to Rs. 60,000, then you will make Rs. 120000/- per annum as profit or free cash.

- **Inactive Investment**—This is all the money that you receive after longer periods of time. Investing in a business and waiting for five to ten years for the returns is an example of an inactive investment. Inactive investment is a plot, a land, or a business that will not produce any cash but will increase in value and when the time comes, can be sold and money generated.

B. Earned Income: Earned income is the money derived from paid work. Majority of people falls into this category. There are two major forms:

- **Pay cheques:** A pay cheque is your monthly or yearly salary derived in the form of a cheque.
- **Commission:** A commission is given in the form of $1 = 1$. If you are a sales representative and sell ten units, you get a commission as a percentage of those ten units. There are various types of commissions.
  - Direct referral commission
  - Trading commission
  - Per conversion commission
  - Sales commission
  - Recurring Commission

But the first one is known to all the employee class as incentive. Commission or incentive is nothing more than a reward for doing something or doing nothing.

C. Passive Income:

When you get paid month by month every month on automated mode, it is called passive income. A system works for you day and night for years to come. This can be in the form of recurring royalties. There are different options for employees, business owners, and investors to earn passive income ranging from multi-level marketing, book royalties, debt funding, licensing, etc. Think about Mr. Wonderful from *Shark Tank*. His deals are usually royalty deals where he takes $1 on every transaction. This is a real-world example of passive income. Passive income is given in the form of **1 = infinity**, which means one product and unlimited deliveries, product never goes out of stock, never expires, you work once, and get paid infinite times.

Here are the various methods through which you can add to your passive income block:

- **Books:** Books are a great way to earn a passive income for generations to come, but you must write only on topics you know well because that's the way you create value for people who want to buy your book. The best part is that you can master any topic you wish before you start writing. Once you write and publish your own book through a publishing house, you will receive royalties as a percentage on every book sold or you can self-publish for a higher percentage of passive income. Grow deeper by creating an e-book, audio book, hard cover, soft cover, etc., and grow wider by creating an online video course, audio/email courses, and speaking in seminars.

- **Franchise:** The franchisor gets royalties for

every franchise that is bought, opened, and functioning. Some people start a business, and show great traction to get franchisees to make passive income in form of royalties. You can find a million examples online as well as around you. Find what you can build well and fast with a great traction report or history, and find people who want to duplicate your success. Invest in advertising to generate leads by advertising on franchisee network or platforms or through brokers.

- **Video Courses:** Create an online course. Create more in the area of your expertise to earn in royalties. Draft your course. Write content based on needs of your audience and learn to market it. It's an amazing source of passive income. You can check for yourself on sites like **Udemy** or **Teachable** how millions of people have bought multiple courses. There are some blueprints to create video courses and create internal content, which I will be sharing with you later.

- **Multi-level Marketing:** This is a great way to earn passive income, learn marketing, develop great communication skills, relationship management, presentation skills, and a lot more. MLM is a system for selling goods and services through a network of direct distributors. Each distributor gets paid for every person he/she adds to the business model. For example: Amway, Avon, Herbal Life, etc. Basically, this income can be called residual income instead of passive income as sometimes you have to put a significant amount of efforts. People think of it as a scam because it is too good to be true and somehow people are not able to trust these kinds of activities because of their belief system. Another reason is that people expect too much too soon which is not the right approach in this business. When you join you must understand it's a profession just like any other profession, which needs some set of skills, and without having those skills you won't be able to make it. Nobody has done it that easily even though they present it lavishly but stories of those leaders who claim to be financially free on the stage are very long and have a history of struggle and consistency. My advice is that you join it for fun and learn the skills, watch the top leaders, observe them, know more about their personal life and thinking process, source of quality information, etc.

- **Software:** Subscription-based business software or an app is simply a terrific way to create passive income on automated mode where money is deducted month by month or every quarter or annually via saved credit cards of the buyers/users. Few examples of this are Netflix, Amazon Prime, Kajabi, Optimize Press, Send Grid, Mail Chimp, etc.

- **Advertising:** Automated advertisements on your website, blogs and YouTube videos via Google AdSense—each time an ad gets clicked or played, you get paid. There are alternatives to Google but still Google has more value for you. If you have no website, blog or videos then look out for something else you can do or write to me about your top three problems and I will post a video for you in answer.

- **Rental:** Rental business can be a very lucrative revenue model to become financially free. Now suppose if you rent a house which has four rooms and you give each room on rent at 20-30% higher rate, then you can see for yourself the monthly free cash flow you'll have. You will also get high security, which can be again invested for the next rental property. It's a very simple game; I suggest if you want to start, then start with a two-unit home and go higher based on your earned experience. I have done it so I know how great this can be for anyone who wishes to generate passive income to become financially free. I have a twelve-month plan for this; you can rent twelve apartments in a year but you only have to invest for the first one. It's simple math; your security is covered double or 1.5x, rent is covered at 20% hike or maybe double in some cases. Rent a flat at 20% lower than the market price around a business hub or colleges, rent it out at 20% or 30% hike per unit (1 room = 1 unit), write it down for the next twelve months and see how much money you can generate; you will have twelve salaries coming in to your account in the thirteenth month.

- **Digital Delivery Products:** These products can't be touched, or held in your hands. The following products are used as a source of passive income. Anyone who is selling and utilizing the products will earn passive income.
  - Website Membership Sites like Shopify, BigRock, HostGator, etc.
  - Apps
  - Social Media Marketing
  - SEO Subscription
  - Blogs - WordPress
  - Templates Sellers and Marketplaces

- **Membership:** Gym, yoga, dance, aerobics, swimming pool, club memberships are all sources of passive income but I don't prefer it.

- **Consultancy:** CAs, lawyers, legal advisers are all examples of consultancies where the service provider earns irrespective of whether a consumer utilizes the services or not. Think what you can offer and to whom? How it will add value to their bank account or in any other means? Consultancy is nothing except using your professional or personal knowledge in a well-organized manner to solve their problems as quickly as possible.

- **Drop-shipping:** The middleman who does not invest in a warehouse, storage, or production, simply makes a profit from connecting users to producers, picking up a product on credit and selling it on 5x to 20x price on Amazon and other platforms. What a drop shipper does is he or she gets in touch with few suppliers or manufacturers of the products he or she wishes to sell online and asks for a demo and asks for a credit period as well, and later, when all the meetings are done, he or she makes a call. Next step, which was already prepared and taken, was to sign up as a seller on Amazon, and the third step is to list the product to sell and go live. Once you are done, you can also drive traffic from Facebook to your product page to sell more units. I have done it in 2013 with a T-shirt and can tell you that you really don't have to do much. Think of it as a book and as a product. I got four orders in three days, one hundred sixty-three in one month, when I uploaded it and went live on a shopping site. My profit was Rs. 400 ($ 6.30 approximately) per T-shirt, and it was growing.

- **Script/Song writing:** Writing a script or writing a song will pay you well if it becomes a hit. The amount of income depends on publicity and how well people receive it. Even a singer makes passive income on a monthly basis. A composer can also sell his compositions, jingles, tunes, and music online. There are so many sites where you can sell MP3s in all the major download stores (iTunes, Amazon, Google, and more). You can get your music on streaming sites like Spotify, Rhapsody, and Deezer. You can find more online.

- **Microfinance:** Lending money on a higher interest rate to those who are not eligible for bank loans or want no hassle in order to get money fast is called microfinancing. Lenders make passive income from the interest rates that are taken on the loans. This is one of my favourite ones as it generates huge income for lenders. I lend money to the lenders and that decreases my hassle with talking to so many people; it saves time and provides higher level of money protection.

- **Licensing:** Patents, copyrights, and product licensing are all examples of methods to earn passive income for a very long period. For example, a copyright on a specific idea, product, or technology can be converted into passive income by the creator. Each time a user uses the idea, product, or technology, you make money. Licensing agreements can be time-bound or quantity-bound. For example, the android platform and internet security softwares, etc.

- **Painting/Photography:** An artist earns passive income each time a painting or photograph is sold or used. An example of this is Shutterstock and other image buying and selling sites where photographers sell their pictures, painters sell their artwork.

- **Leasing:**
  - **Car Lease:** Some asset management companies lease cars to other multimillion dollar companies for their highly paid top management staff. These agreements are made for three to five years, and the companies make 2x, 3x, or even 4x money

than what they pay to banks in EMIs, and later on they sell those cars. How it works is this: these people first take orders from the companies and then buy new cars based on their requirements and roll it up. What I figured out that if you are serious then you can find a way to make anything an asset and turn it into passive income.

o **Office Lease:** This one is simple and most awesome, even a kid can do it. In a growing start-ups economy, there is huge demand for co-working spaces and dedicated plug and play offices. Nowadays, many co-working offices lease out a single desk or office cabins for a certain amount of deposit and monthly rental. The nature of the game is same as I mentioned in rental properties.

• **Lockers:** People don't prefer to keep moving their secret wealth again and again but they look for safety and security for their precious items. They look for most secure lockers in town provided by banks or private companies. For such facilities, banks and private security companies ask for a fixed rental that can be high or average. Another example of locker facilities income is schools and clubs as they also charge and earn passive income.

- **Warehouses:** It seems small but creates more for a long time. As part of their expansion plans, so many e-commerce companies look for warehouses to store their products. If you have a space, be it small or big, then all you need to do is put up an ad on top five classified platforms and optimize it or hire a broker.

- **Reward or Penalty:** Why are banks mostly always profitable? Because they never lose what they get. A bank or a NBFC will make money when you make money or you lose money, but how? By asking customers to maintain a certain amount in an account or else pay penalties. If you maintain any amount, they invest it and earn. If you don't maintain then you have no choice but to pay penalties. This is how banks earn passive income from their bank accounts. It's a game of Reward or Penalty.

- **Telephone towers:** Certain buildings get paid for hosting telephone towers on their roofs. My ex-girlfriend had one on her rooftop and was paid Rs. 1,00,000 per month for it. I asked her how she went about it, and she told me that they approached few telecom companies and since there was no tower around and that was one of the reasons for poor network and call drops, people from the various companies came, checked the location, and one said yes.

- **ATMs:** All Time Money for bank customers and monthly passive income for you. If you have a small space at a good location then you can think of utilizing this plan. It's better than having a tenant as it means higher rent.
- **Parking Lots:** Misunderstood, underestimated, and undervalued business idea because what people see is upfront poor people managing the parking, but I have never seen any poor or middle-class person owning any parking lot in a good location. It's the business of rich people. A one-time investment that earns daily depending on the number of cars that park in the lot. If it is your own parking lot, built on your own land, then you have a pot of gold.
- **Merchandize (vending machines):** One-time efforts can pay over and over in the form of passive income once installed. A vending machine makes passive income for the installer of the machine; on top of that refills are like the cherry on top. If you tie up with a brand or launch your own, you need to find corporate, gyms, clubs, spas, salons, etc.
- **Affiliate Marketing:** This is a type of performance-based marketing. Payment is made for each visitor depending on the affiliate and his marketing techniques. How

does it work? Well, you sign up for an affiliate program on any affiliate network or your favourite website, if they have an affiliate program. A link will be created with your reference ID, which you can share using mailers, social media posts, direct marketing, etc. As soon as a sale happens, you will make some commission. Some affiliates have recurring commission for their promoters/affiliate marketers and some save cookies for a month. You can roam around a bit and start a professional course on ClickBank and JVzoo; they are the best for this.

- **Newspapers/Magazine Subscription:** A newspaper or magazine earns passive income depending on the number of users of the product or service that is being marketed.

- **Apps:** Transactional apps are the best way to earn money easily with less work and with almost no employees. We have more than twenty apps under different brand names on Google Play. Some of them are freemium and some of them are subscription based. It's super easy and one of the fastest ways to generate passive income. Here are some revenue methods we are using: ads revenue, affiliate ads inside the apps, one-time purchases and subscriptions. You don't need a huge app; this can be very small but highly useful for the market.

- **Software:** Web-based software subscription plans are a super popular way to generate lifelong income, but your income depends on your market and how you are going to market it. You can hire a development team inhouse or outsource it.

In order to generate multiple streams of income and run them successfully, there are also certain parameters for choosing a Passive Income Business for everlasting growth and it should not demand much time every day or all the days of the week from you. If you have an idea or you have already started to build a business, the first thing for you to do is to test the idea.

Here are some steps to determine whether a business is doable or not based on my personal experiences:

○ **Idea Testing:** Is your idea going to solve a problem of millions or billions? If you want to be a millionaire or a billionaire then you have to find a social problem of 10 million people; the ratio being 1:10. If you want to be a billionaire, then find a problem of 10 billion people. Even if you use this ratio as 1:5, it would work well to make you a millionaire or a billionaire.

- **System:** The business must have a system where you do not have to invest more than twenty-four hours a month or a maximum of hundred hours. Try to stick to the twenty-four hours routine though; but as you work this out, your approach will change and you will find some secret and extremely wise strategies, and your productivity will skyrocket.

  It should always be a system that works for you rather than you working for the system or in the system. You just need to think about income all the time. A system produces income on automated mode even when you are sleeping or when you are on a holiday.

- **Fast:** It should not take time for transactions to take place or close the sale or deliver the product or grant the access.

- **Scalable:** Is it scalable?

  Can you take it from Level 1 to Level 100, can you deliver the product instantly as soon as you receive a sale? Can you go from 100 sales to 1000000 in next ten hours or twenty-four hours, can your infrastructure or server take that kind of load?

- **Profitable:** Define your margins, if your margins are tiny then your business won't survive. Big margins and huge number of sales will make your business worth millions or billions.

— **Small Margins** (5%-20%) = not worth investing

— **Average Margins** (40% and over) = worthwhile

— **Big Margins** (60% and above) I personally do not even think about margins that are less than 70%. I don't prefer such businesses even if it seems like huge volume in customers or sales. It's better to work on big margin products and sell it in volume good enough to make any amount you set as a target.

○ **Addictive:**

— Is it as addictive as an interesting game?

— How can your users love it instead of getting frustrated and leave you?

○ **Viral Factor:** Ask yourself why people or your users will share it? What will make them share your business links, videos, or any other type of content? Why? Quality of top-grossing companies are that they don't have advertising factors because they have viral factors. Look at Google, Facebook,

Apple, Microsoft, Amazon, eBay, Oracle, or any other Fortune 500 company, you will find some great viral factors.

— Can be either negative or positive.
— You do not need to put much marketing muscle into your plan.

o **Self-dependency:** A business should be self-dependent or else you must have a strong and trustworthy backup plan all the time. Just because I ignored this, I lost $2 million with an ongoing growth rate of 960% annually. So, it's better to learn a hard lesson the easy way rather than facing hard times when things are going the easy way.

o **Self-sustainability:** A business must be self-sustainable without outside funding and that comes with huge margins and a rockstar product, which sells itself in enough quantity.

o **Kind of Product:** What products, services, or programs are you trying to bring to the market? What niche does it have? Find out below:

o **Under Niche**
— Less demand
— Limited audience

o **Upper Niche:** This is where fortune is.

- — Huge audience
- — Depends on how you market it
- ○ **Brand new**
  - — New invention
  - — Need to educate audience
  - — Need to create new market
- ○ **Manpower**
  - — The more manpower you have, the less profit you make
  - — Re-think if the business requires a lot of manpower
- ○ **Product Customer Ratio**
  - — If your product or service or program has to be produced for each customer separately, it is the 1:1 ratio. If you have one product that can be delivered to millions or billions of users, then it is called 1:Infinite ratio.

#7. Portfolio Income:

These are fundable assets that you have acquired or invested in. Simple examples of this are stocks, bonds, and even land. When you can take funding against assets, this becomes a portfolio income.

Here are examples of portfolio income:

- • **Stocks**
- • **Bonds**

- **Dividends**
- **Insurance**
- **Properties**
- **Leverage After Investment**

What is Leverage?

Leverage is tapping into the full potential of the money you have or you can have. For example, if you have 10000 customers but you are selling only one product to them, then you can't call it leverage, but if you find out their categories, industries, then you can figure out their problems. In further process, you can sell a number of products, which can solve their problems. As a result, you will leverage your data.

- Leveraging is an investment strategy where borrowed money or borrowed capital is used to increase the potential return of an investment.
- High leverage means more debt than equity.
- Thus, leverage could also refer to the amount of debt used to finance assets.
- Margins: Borrowed money used to invest in other financial institutions. Thus, margins are used to create leverage.
- Leverage: Making sure that the investment is growing without using personal money.

CHAPTER 6

LIVE A FINANCIALLY REWARDING LIFE

Now that you know how to build a strong financial foundation, how to start working on your dreams, how to have a mindset of success, how to acquire required skills to be extraordinary in your space, how to plan for an income, and how to earn money, it's time to put your money to work. Use your money as a system, rather as a business system, which can produce automated income, and decide to live a financially rewarding life forever.

A rewarding life can be possible only on one term and that is when you focus on rewards—the first rule of an investment is that an investment has to be rewarding. Outcome of an investment is a reward: the more you invest, the better rewards you get, but whilst wisely following ground rules of the investment game. It doesn't matter where you are, you can find ways to invest your money and make more money. Take baby steps, start from somewhere even if you have a chance of getting a bit hurt. Don't start anything with a negative approach because that changes your attitude, emotions, thoughts, behaviour, and finally results. Nothing is negative and nothing is positive, the simple thumb rule is 'whatever works, works'. And never forget your mantra to be successful 'whatever it takes'. Do whatever it takes to be successful because it will return your pride, the one and only parameter of measuring success is money, your valuation, your net worth. Do whatever it takes, learn whatever skills it takes, give whatever it takes, and create passive income for yourself and your loved ones.

Basic Rules Of Investment

Before you can begin investing money, it is essential to understand and implement some basic rules of investment. Anybody with basic knowledge can invest money and generate passive income if they focus, calculate, and take action. The process of moving from an employee or self-employed status to a business owner or a sophisticated investor is like a caterpillar transforming into a butterfly— it takes time and requires a complete change in mindset and behaviour. The most important change is to understand what to do with the money that is now at your disposal. Do you spend it like you used to before or do you intelligently invest in? The choice is yours.

If you choose to invest your money wisely, here are some basic rules to master to become a sophisticated investor by understanding and taking baby steps.

Rule #1: Know what kind of income you're working for

Most people only think and know about working income, but they never consider that there are different kinds of incomes that they are working for. **Ordinary earned income** is the money that you make from working a 9-5 job and where you pick up a paycheque. The ability to earn is directly related to the number of hours that you can work. **Portfolio income** is earned through paper assets like stocks, bonds, dividends, and insurance policies. **Passive income** is derived from real estate, royalties, and other mediums I already mentioned in chapter 5.

The main difference is the amount of tax that is taken from these three kinds of income. Earned income is taxed the highest, which leaves a lower amount of disposable income. Passive income has multiple tax exemptions and hence this kind of income leaves a higher amount of disposable income. The advice is that if you want a higher amount of free cash, work for passive income and portfolio income as compared to earned income. Remember this, *salaries are always lower than royalties.*

Rule #2: Convert ordinary income into passive income

Most individuals start out in life by drawing salaries as an employee. However, what makes them shift to a business owner or investor is the knowledge that there are other types of income. Think about it like this—you go to an ice-cream shop and purchase the same flavour because they have only one flavour (vanilla). One day, you walk into the shop and are pleasantly surprised because they now have a range of flavours for you to choose from. There are some people who would play it safe and still choose vanilla whereas some individuals would take a risk and try the other flavours that are available. How many of you stayed in the same hotel twice, thrice, or multiple times because you are afraid of new experience and love comfort and predictability? I choose a different hotel every time.

The reason why I gave you those two examples is because if you get scared of new experiences or shifting and can't take smaller risks, then you do not deserve to make BIG money. My advice is to convert ordinary income to passive income since this leaves the most amounts of free cash for you to use. This is the only path to building wealth. Imagine that you get a pay raise or more cash flow from product sales as a business owner, what would you do with it? The intelligent thing to do is to pay yourself, take out some percentage as you decided through chapter 5 and then invest that money in cash-flowing assets. The advantage of investing in cash-flowing assets is that your money is not bound and will be paid with return rate in a shorter period of time. Hence, converting ordinary income into passive income is the next step to becoming a great investor. To be great or call yourself great, you don't have to be famous; you just need to make wise decisions for yourself, I mean passive income producing decisions. If you can't turnaround your own life then later on definitely you won't be great, you won't be able to create and leave behind a legacy. Greatness comes from within by doing your best every time . . . again and again.

Rule #3: The investor is an asset or a liability

It is essential to understand that it is not the investment that is risky but the decision maker of that investment deal because your decision can be an asset or a liability; it can't be both. The third step to being a good investor is to invest in financial education, which is not taught in schools or colleges. Find unique content, approaches that allow an individual to understand the intricacies of finance and the economy. Then, start small, avoid mistakes in the first place but if you make them, then learn to learn from your mistakes because nothing can replace real-life experience. Once you are attuned to the environment of investing, then start making bigger and bigger investments. But always remember, if you are the investor, you are the asset or liability, not your investment.

Rule #4: Be prepared

If you are not prepared with education, experience, and extra cash, a good opportunity will pass you by. Hence, it is always important to be prepared for whatever may come your way. My advice here is to not predict what will happen, but to stay focused on what you want. Keep your eyes open to what is happening and respond to the investment environment. A good investor is always prepared. Every opportunity you miss that's a cost to your financial independence.

Rule #5: Learn to evaluate risk and reward

Just like every company does a SWOT analysis to understand and solve major problems, it is important to learn how to evaluate risk and reward. My method is simple: do not invest until you do not understand well enough to make it an asset. Protection of invested money, high returns, monthly passive income, control over investment, that's all basics but top traits you need to know.

Start with an Account

My sole advice when you begin investing is to open an account and if you do not trust yourself with the money then do not get a debit card or a chequebook. What this does is that it inhibits you from recklessly spending your hard-earned money. In order to make transactions, you would have to go to the bank and this would be a longer process than simply signing a chequebook or swiping your card. It has been found that such transactions are fewer as compared to cheque and card transactions. If you want to become a good investor and earn from your investments, do not opt in for a card or chequebook facility. I did this myself and opted for a bank with very few branches across India. Here are some highly valuable steps to your fortunes:

#1. Capture—What you want

Identify the possible options that are available for you to invest in. If you are just starting out, it is intelligent to follow good investors and study their patterns of investment. It is also essential to get an education in finance to be able to make your own decisions and choices about investment. Only learn from quality people who are self-made in any space because they are built on a real-life foundation through tough times. Further, it is important to gain some first-hand experience as well. Thus, the first step is to be prepared and then **identify** all the possible avenues for investment. Capture your areas of interest for passive income. Capture what you want, all dreams, where you wish to be successful as an investor. Write down everything that can make you rich, whether you know it or you don't.

#2. Filter—What you know best

Once you have identified all the possible investment opportunities, **filter those on the basis of your skills and best abilities**. If your next question is how to filter opportunities, the answer is simple: only invest in those opportunities that you can understand. It is stupid to invest in a tech company just because it is doing well even though you have no technological know-how. You will not be able to understand the trends and will not know when to withdraw or increase your investment. Start small, start simple with baby steps. Filter your possibilities and invest only in those that you have a keen understanding of.

#3. Analyze—What you can achieve faster

The next step is to **closely analyze** the options that you have filtered. This means weighing the risks and rewards. If you invest without analyzing, you are in for big trouble. Would you enrol in a course without understanding the benefits that the course would accrue? Would you join a company without asking the salary and benefits of the same? No. Thus, do not invest without analyzing. It is fairly simple: look at trends, check reviews, and use your common sense and experience to make a decision of whether the opportunity is investible or not.

#4. Invest—Decide to invest

After you have captured, filtered, and analyzed the investible opportunities, it is now time to begin **investing**. As mentioned before, start small and simple, investing in opportunities based on trends and risk-reward analysis. It is essential that you understand the investing environment and withdraw or increase investments based on how your investment performs in any other sector, any business you are in for passive income and profits.

#5. Protect—Protection before Investment

Find ways to protect your principal amount and make sure money flows from passive income. When I started out, I invested in micro-financing and I lost my principal amount and some passive interest as well. I tried again and lost again, and then I decided not to trust everybody, but to bind everybody through somebody and with some other mediums.

#6. Multiply

This is #AwesomeSauce. Here, you create layer above layer, reward on reward, interest on interest for years and years to come. Your wealth grows like anything if done the right way. Stop eating your rewards of investment and invest the rewards and repeat. Keep it until the seventh generation of rewards, and then you can use it. Make sure you multiply a passive income out of your investments made for years and years.

#7. Repeat

When you are attuned to investing, protecting and multiplying, you can freely **repeat** the process and you will be on the path to becoming a great investor for sure. I guarantee your success if you follow the steps mentioned in this whole book. I can, because if it has worked for me from zero to a million, then it can work for anybody. If a flight can take me from New Delhi to New York, the same flight can take you there.

Types of Income: where to invest?

It is essential to understand the types of income that will give you an idea of where to invest. Write it to see how much you know or you need to learn and enhance your skills to have a better future.

List 25 Businesses To Invest In

Name of the Business	Advantages to you

Name of the Business	Advantages to you

CHAPTER 7

BUILD A FINANCIAL BACKBONE

When the whole world was suffering through the 2008 financial crisis, India was growing rapidly, and that financial crisis did not leave any bad impact on our economy. Most countries and people don't know—

-What has saved us?
-What saved us from economical fall?

Well, it was a habit, our habit of saving money. Indian people have this tendency to save money for bad times. If you have never seen tough times then you were born with a silver spoon—good for you! But for most of us, living the middle-class or poor class life, a bad time does come without any prior notice. In India, 30-40% people also know how to utilize savings in good times. We don't let our money sit idle in a cupboard or in any bank account. Although saving money won't make you rich, but it will have so many psychological long-term effects, which you will come to know once you start saving money. I will give you a glimpse of how do I save and how my savings are making me richer.

Paying less for something is not the saving, neither is keeping that money in your saving account. Value of any saved amount should grow higher even if inflation rate goes higher, and the rate of inflation will definitely go higher each year. So, as the inflation rate goes higher, you lose purchasing power and that's how saving in legitimate currency is a bad idea. But you can turn it into a positive opportunity.

To cut to the solution, you can buy gold and/or silver. Why do I buy gold and silver coins every week? Gold has been highly rewarding for the last five years, average return on income is more than 20% in India, Last year I made 30% on my savings. If you are from any other country, you can Google ROI on gold investment in your country. Take baby steps, even if you have $10 or $50, start buying gold coins, just avoid paying making charges because you are going to invest on weekly and monthly basis for a really long time. Once you buy the gold or silver, three things will happen:

1. You have something tangible that will grow in purchasing value against dollar or rupees.
2. The gold/silver you have will be equal to having no money so you won't even think to spend it as you would have done with the dollar or rupees notes; this is great for those who can't trust themselves with cash.

3. If needed, without selling your gold, you can easily walk in to any bank and get a gold loan, and on top of everything, you can invest that loan amount. Somewhere, you are sure that it is protected and returns are definitely way high after deducting your interest rates or fee and in total your ROI is somewhere between 30% to 45% annually. If you pick a paper and a pen and start exploring this single discussion then you will find out something magical. There are certain things which we won't say on stage or in a book as an authority, so consider it your homework. Make your brains outperform on this topic!

Later, in six or twelve months, you can explore the options to save money into dividends or tax-free bonds.

SAVINGS

The dictionary definition of the word saving is to prevent the waste of a particular resource. Similarly, the purpose of savings is to prevent the waste of the 'purchasing value of money'. I personally believe that saving is extremely important because it allows an individual to measure the value of money.

Why to save?

Saving helps you control your mind and expenditure. We spend on unnecessary things, but you will only realize after analysis that you are overspending. An example of controlling expenditure is cutting down on unhealthy food that makes you gain weight and later on you pay a personal trainer or a doctor to lose the same weight. How intelligent is that? Instead, buy healthier options that are bound to be cheaper and will also ensure that you do not fall sick or gain weight. Saving is also helpful to make more money. In India, the annual return on saving is 4-6% and inflation rate revolves around 5-11%. So, ultimately you lose money by giving away your purchasing power unknowingly. Hence, save so that you can make more money from your savings. If your question is how to make more on your savings, the answer could be as simple as maintaining an envelope to collect and keep an amount to be saved, and then multiply.

Here are seven tips to save money:

1. Do not keep change in your wallet. Like I don't keep a note below Rs. 500 ($7.50 approx.) with me. If I get it, then I put it in an envelope/drawer at the end of the day.
2. Save daily on things if you can easily, but do not spend much time on it.

3. Save money when you get a pay cheque or through other means as you decided: 10% to 20%; check chapter 5.
4. Do not avoid saving, do not save the money to just keep it as a prisoner but to build your purchasing value through gold and silver.
5. Protect 100% of what you have saved, don't lose it.
6. Do not use your saving amount directly but use the amount, which your savings have generated in additional purchasing value.
7. Keep saving until your expenses come down to 10% or 15% of your total income, then you can feel free to manipulate it a bit, and you will only achieve that status if you focus on earnings, investments, savings, and controlling your expenses till the time you hit the status.

What is Good Saving?

Good saving is what makes you money. The only rule in good saving is to never let your money sit idle. An example of what you can do is inspired by my real-life activities: after saving money every month, I invested this money in buying gold. Each month I would buy some gold and keep saving it for the future. Then, I realized that during Diwali, as the demand for gold increases, the price also shoots up. I then decided to sell the gold during

Diwali time at a profit of 20%. This seemed like a pretty good profit. I also realized that once Diwali passes, the demand falls and the prices fall too. I bought back the gold I had sold and repeated the process each Diwali. This way I made money off my savings through gold. Another thing I did with the gold was that I never let it rest. I gave the gold to a jeweller and got 100% as a loan. Then, I decided to put this money in microfinance and got a 25-30% profit. Overall, my total return was 45-50%. Once you understand how to use gold as good savings, you can find other materials like silver, copper to use to earn money from your savings. Another option is to find products in demand. Then, find sellers willing to sell at a cost lower than the market cost and find buyers willing to buy at a price higher than the market price. In this way, you can use the economy to earn some profit through your savings.

Let me tell you what I did, I call it the stockout strategy. I won't prefer to name it but a very fashionable shopping site in India has amazing and only branded items; they run mega sales or on-and-off promotions with up to 90% discounts. I choose shirts from top brands and check how many pieces are remaining in their stock. I add all and buy at bottom prices. One thing I know that whatever goes out of stock on this site, doesn't come back for two to six months, so I sell the same stuff at 30% discount on the same site or other sites. Branded items are always in demand and even if it sells slow, I still multiply my savings. Using my stockout strategy, I made around $1874 in profit in two months approximately. You can find so many ways to multiply your savings and make additional income at no cost with fewer efforts.

What is a Bad Saving?

Most people do this as they keep saving and don't touch their savings. Their logic is that they save for bad times. But, such money is a liability because it doesn't make you more money. For an individual, saving that is just kept is a liability as it makes them more paranoid—more locks, more security. But, for a bank, this liability is converted into profits as the bank usually loans out such money. The learning here is to not just keep the money but to invest it or even loan it out. Bad saving is something that you should avoid by primarily using the tactics of good saving mentioned above. Another point is that you should be able to cash out your savings immediately if needed so you can follow my ways to make it work or you can look out for profitable opportunities.

When to Save?

Whenever you get money, whenever you receive any amount, you must save. The rule is so simple: first save, then think about spending. A fixed percentage of your earned income should be saved on the payday. As for paycheques, save on day one, before you spend a single penny. The wise thing to do is divide your paycheque into four parts: investments, saving, spending, and emergency using the blueprint explained before. The only advice is: save on payday, not once you are done with all your expenditures because nothing will be left to save then.

These are the four things you must do once you receive your paycheque:

1. Put money aside for savings: if you wait for the end of the month to save, there will probably be nothing left to save. One suggestion to solve this problem is to directly deposit a percentage of your paycheque into a savings account. This way you will not be tempted to spend all of it before you save.

2. Allocate money for your expenses: make sure that your paycheque supports all your expenses till the next time you get paid. The best way to do this is to initially allocate money for all your expenses and ensure that you do not overspend.

3. Figure out what is due and when: make sure that you pay your dues on time to prevent any stressful situations. Make a list of all that is due and when for a smooth financial planning.

4. Make sure your important expenses are covered: sometimes, in buying the things we want, we ignore the things we need. Ensure that your important expenses are covered first by your paycheque, and after saving, you can then spend, but not splurge on the things that you want.

Save Daily

Before I did this, I did not believe that this habit was so magical. I decided that I won't carry change lower than Rs. 500 in my wallet, so as soon as I got to my apartment, I used to put that money aside in an envelope. When a habit becomes regular, it will become an asset. Till today, I do not have any bills of less than Rs. 500 in my wallet. At the end of the month, I had saved Rs. 13,000 using this single method, plus the payday amount was separate. Then, I decided to try it for another few months. At the end of three months, I had about Rs. 50000+ in total. I decided to invest this money and made a significant amount of profit from the same method I mentioned. Remember that this is free saving. This money is not needed elsewhere and will not make any difference in your day-to-day life. Once you make this a habit, it will become an asset because at the end of the month, you will invest this money. The point here is just to save; what you will do with the money will come to you later. It's about forming successful habits. Small and tiny habits will make huge impacts in your life.

Life is about living, not cutting down on your costs, I prefer to earn more and live my life to the fullest. Yes, I admit that for few months or a year or two, we can compromise and build our income, assets, rather than going through our entire life being a victim by surviving, suffering, and not living at all.

Make it an asset

Fix a time every month when you check your saving account and make whatever you have saved into an asset by investing it after a given period of time. Think how and where you can protect it and multiply it.

Hold it

People usually spend their savings on unnecessary things or on shopping. Hold on to your savings even if you are tempted to, and you feel that you need to spend it. You need to learn and form all the habits that will work for you, in your favour. Saving is saving, not to be spent. Do not spend a single penny from your savings for the first six months at least. Then you can use the additional purchasing power you have created out of those savings.

Treat Yourself

Hold all the savings and any sort of return on saving; do not touch it for six months. Whatever interest or reward you get out of your savings as an outcome, after three to six months, it is now time to treat yourself. Personally, I donate stuff or buy things for students, because in India life is really hard for rural students. They have no chairs, no ACs, no washrooms, no quality education to speak of, and I like to play my part in bettering that for them in whichever way I can.

The point is you can do whatever you like with your savings, treat yourself if that makes you happy or treat others if that makes you happy.

CHAPTER 8

SPEND AS IF YOU ARE BROKE

Once you divide your income into investment, savings, and emergency, the remaining amount should be dedicated to expenditure. Spending is all the money that you use to buy products and services. It is essential to understand that there are different types of spending as well. There is expenditure on the things that you most definitely need—these are the essentials for daily living. Then, there is expenditure on the things that you want or you wish to use—these are items that are not essentials but are important to you. Finally, there is expenditure that is unnecessary.

Top Tips:

- Spend only on things which are necessary to live, understand that the more you spend the more you pay in indirect taxes—that's how your maximum income goes towards paying taxes without you realizing it.

- Your total expenses should never be more than 40% of your current income. Initially you can start with 60% for the next one year or six months, and during this period increase your income.
- With lower expenses (and high income), higher the chances of your financial freedom.
- Spend on needs, not what you want in the moment because later on you will have to sell what you need at the price of what you want. I have gone through this as well.
- Stop spending on garbage, junk, which makes you unhealthy—that's a double charge, a big one. You might not realize now but I know it very well.
- Spend on skills rather than activities, an example of this is instead of being a dance student, become a dance trainer, instead of gym, spend on learning martial arts or becoming a black belt trainer. Think differently.

#1. Budget your expenses

Practice the habit of thinking before spending. You can do this by listing down your expenses, marking it with whether you need, want, or can live without that product. It is important to allocate a budget of where to spend and how to spend. Budget doesn't mean that you have to buy things at a cheaper price or less in quantity or compromise with the quality; it means you need to buy things which matter to you, your family, your health. If you avoid it today, tomorrow it will make you cry. Initially, it will be difficult to list down but think what can be more difficult than being bankrupt!

#2. Control

Cut down on unnecessary expenses on things that you can live without. If you feel like something is a habit, ensure that you engage in habit replacement. A simple example of this is if you spend unnecessary money on alcohol because it has become a habit, instead spend money on books or CDs of TV shows that help you spend your time in a better manner, things which can help you to increase your earning abilities and capabilities.

#3. Define your needs and wants

Needs are necessities like food, water, clothing, and shelter. These are the things that you cannot live without. Wants are those things that you do not necessarily need, but desire. It could be an upgraded version of a need or simply something that you would like to have. In order to define your needs and wants, and decide which products to buy, you can ask the following questions:

What does the product satisfy: a need or a want?

How will this product be helpful in my growth?

If you feel that the product does not do much to help you grow and it is a want, then you should refrain from purchasing the product.

#4. Be a seller

This is hard, but in business you can always try to scratch the ground instead of buying something; think of a barter of what is less valuable to you but more valuable to them. Whenever I get a chance to pay, I try to find out whether the seller needs something that I can fulfil. For example, if the seller needs business or financial consultancy, advice on digital media or whatever else my company can provide, I try to make a barter deal with them instead of paying them money. This not only creates a higher value for the seller, it also enables me to save that money. The standard rule here is that buyers never make money, sellers do.

#5. Turn the 'want money' to a saving account

Instead of buying a want that is not required, put the money in your bank account or in an envelope at the end of the day. Like one day I wanted to pay a bill at a five-star hotel where my friend and I had gone for dinner. However, my friend did not let me pay. So, at the end of the day, I put that 'want money' into my saving account. It is as simple as that. Whenever and however that 'want money' is saved, just save it. These habits don't make any big difference but until you are working on financial freedom plan, every small thing will count and contribute to your growth. As of now I don't care about a $100 bill or even $500, neither do I save it because my expenses are lower than 10% of my income and that is where you have to reach by taking the small steps and big steps which I have taken.

#6. Rules of spending

If you spend on prostitution, gambling, whims that are fired by impulses, emotional spending on days like Valentine's day, luxury buying like a boat cruise, and not needed things like extra clothes, you will always be poor. The time might be right, but if your habits are wrong, you will never become rich. Ensure that you recognize habits that control you, and always think before spending.

Break the bad habits: be conscious about what you eat, drink, and stop spending on junk which will make you sick and get you hospitalized.

CHAPTER 9

MASTER THE DEBT MONSTER

Debt is a sum of money that is owed or due—it is all the money that you have borrowed and pending payments on you. It's a boon and a curse both. It's a small or big leak which can sink a ship of your success, it can rob you, it can trouble you, it can take away your mental peace, it can drain your earning potential, it can waste your efforts, and finally it can destroy you if you don't use it wisely and if you don't get rid of it.

I call it a debt monster because it has ruined millions of lives and still millions are under attack. Millions of people are living paycheque to paycheque and cannot find ways out, and are hence frustrated, depressed, desperate, de-motivated, financially paralyzed, and stuck very badly. Some people think that their salaries will be enough to pay off their debt, and that they will collect the sum over a period of time and pay it off. This is not a smart move because if you put all your money to pay off debts, you will not even be able to think about investment. If you cannot think about investing, you cannot think about becoming financially free. If you have a million dollars today, it won't last long as cost of living is getting higher and on top of that you also have to keep some for emergency. But if you invest 60-80% of that million dollars, it will last very long.

When you are deeply in debt, you are not just frustrated, desperate, or stressed, but you also lose self-worth, self-respect, and highly valuable relationships. Only people who have been dead-broke will be able to relate to this because not everybody's strength, certainty, mindset, and everything else they have got, are tested.

A common man, when he gets his salary, does only two things: goes and spends it on shopping and then tries to save. Even if they have free cash, they do not invest. However, this is the biggest problem with people who face financial crises. In this chapter, you will learn how to get rid of debt, the different types of debts, and how to make money from debt. But what is essential to understand first is that you should always keep money aside to invest in the first place. This is what will save you even when you are in a big debt. Save yourself from a debt attack as countries save themselves from attacks—just think how countries are prepared to avoid wars, protect themselves and attack back. At the end of the day, it's all about staying strong financially.

In addition to investing, one should always have a financial buffer (emergency account) for all those emergencies and rainy days. A financial buffer is an additional amount to account for unforeseen expenses that can arise now and then for all individuals. Many people do not have enough to save, spend and invest, and thus a buffer is a very far-off concept for them. It's not okay if you do not manage an emergency account because if you fall, and chances are you will, you will take 10x or 20x time to get back but if you have this financial buffer or an emergency account, whatever you call it, you can rise up faster, you can build your empire quickly, you can save yourself from suffering and poor survival. I have gone through this phase where I had to lay low for a few months because all my money was going towards paying large sum EMIs, and I had nothing in my emergency account. Sometimes, even when you have the earning potential, you won't be able to earn an income in real life because of lack of funds in the circulation or some hard circumstances. There are no excuses for your success or for not proceeding, but it might get delayed, and nothing will fall as per your plan for one simple reason: **when you have no money, you lose control over things that can reproduce for you some great income or fortunes or even a survival.**

Here are the essential steps to attain financial freedom:

- **Understand your starting point:** Before you decide where you want to go, it is essential to know where you stand now. Do this by calculating your net worth. If your net worth is going down, then you are in a risky position and are getting less wealthy. But if your net worth is increasing, then you are going towards being financially free.

Net worth = Assets − Debts

Write down all positive cash flow income from assets and subtract all debts. It's a great idea to perform at least once for yourself. See how those numbers will make you feel.

- **Track your spending:** Successfully managing cash flow is the key to financial freedom, but building a strong financial plan requires understanding how much you spend and save each year. The point of this is to see whether you end the year cash positive (surplus) or cash negative (deficit). You can create a monthly routine check on a paper. Do everything whatever matters to your life, every small thing matters if it can have a big impact in your career and life.

  A small leakage is big enough to kill all the people on the ship.

  So, track your spending or earn so much that you don't even have to care about it ever in life.

- **Adjust your spending:** This is where you look closer at your spending to check whether you are spending more or less than your income. It is essential to have a cash surplus in order to attain your goals. If you are not in a cash surplus, you have to adjust and change your spending habits by probably cutting down on things you do not really need.

As soon as you get more money, a fake need zone is created by your mind to test your abilities, capabilities, and disabilities whether you can handle and keep more if given or not, so don't lose your consciousness and golden chance to stay rich.

- **Set your life goals:** think of what type of life you want in the future, and how you are going to organize your life now to get it. Financial goals do not just happen, you have to make them happen by changing your actions now to influence the future. You can do this by imagining where you want to be five years down the line and plan, organize, and behave in a way that will take you to that position. You can also go though some step-by-step exercises to know what life you truly want and deserve. Remember, books are the best, greatest investment and gifts, which you can stock for your kids and other family members. I can ask you to do so because that's what I have been doing for a long time.

- **Develop a strategy:** The key here is to maintain timelines and develop strategies to make your goals materialize. In order to do this, you need a plan. Mainly, aim to spend less and earn more. You can do this by cutting down on things you do not need and finding additional sources of income as well. You can find so many small or big earning opportunities easily nowadays. For instance, if you have a small debt of $500 then you can find a high-cost product like watches, perfumes, suites, etc., and sell only one or two or ten units of it to make a profit of $500. Write down action steps that you plan on taking to attain your goal—this is your strategy.

- **Create your final plan:** A typical financial plan should have five parts:
  - Where you stand financially—your current situation in earnings.
  - Where you want to go—how much you need to earn?
  - Net worth statement—what is your net worth? Subtract debts from assets income.
  - Steps you must take to achieve your goals—what you are going to sell to cover or repay the debt?
  - Investment Policy statement that defines how your portfolio is to be invested—how are you going to build your portfolio for a great future? What are you going to invest in?

    Writing down your thoughts is worth a lot and you should start exercising your brain to have more clarity about the destination you wish to reach because if you don't know where you want to be, you will never get there.

Let's understand all major sides of bad debt, good debt, and how to get rid of it and how to leverage it for higher income.

What is Bad Debt?

Bad debt is the kind of debt that you do not make any money out of. When you use debt for your personal expenses, when you save debt amount, when you treat debt as your income, When you pay your debt with another debt, this will create a mess in your life—this is bad debt. Now suppose if you have invested, spent, or saved that debt amount and somehow it doesn't create more income than you are liable to pay to your lenders in the form of EMIs or interest with principal amount; that's a mess and a bad debt. Simple definition of bad debt is: **a bad debt will put you in more debt.**

If you are not making more than the interest payment for the debt, that is bad debt. When you do not utilize or manage your debt well, that is bad debt. You will face a definite financial crisis because of your bad debt if your earnings are not enough to pay the debt. Yes. Read that again.

The first step to prevent a financial crisis is to hold the money from the debt rather than spending it. The only way you can hold onto money is by forming good habits and management skills. Sometimes, people do not know how to use debt, merely because they are not financially educated or mature enough. In this case, they should take the help they require to understand how to utilize the money from debt.

When you spend the money that you have taken as a debt, but it does not make you any money further, this will lead to more and more debt. With a web of debt come various problems. Usually, **debt drains out your energy and diverts your focus**. If you focus on making money rather than what your actual job is, if you put in more energy in handling debt than making money, you are in for big trouble. Additional to this is when people chase you to pay off your debt—that is embarrassing. You know what I mean. So, it's way better to plan ahead, stop treating debt as your income, and make more money out of it by using your investment or sales skills.

What is Good Debt?

Capture	Numbers	Sell Total
Debt Amount		
What product/service can you sell to pay off the first debt?		
Buying Price		
Selling Price		

Capture	Numbers	Sell Total
Cost to acquire a Customer		
Net Profit		
Required Sales Quantity		

Good debt is the money that is spent on income generating assets to create monthly cash flow instantly before you pay your first EMI or interest. It's better to plan how you are going to leverage debt or liabilities before you even get it because it's always better to be prepared when you have no opportunities rather having an opportunity and not be prepared. The reason behind that thought is: your mind works better under stress and you have more time to think over and over about that idea, you get time to analyze an opportunity and act wisely.

'A good debt will earn you more profit after deducting its own all expenses.'

How to get rid of bad debt?

Pick a paper and a pen to make a list of your debts in ascending order.

1. Assign the name of the person you have borrowed from.
2. What amount have you borrowed?
3. What amount you need to earn next month?

4. What products or services or program you can get to sell through any manufacturer, supplier, or trader? You can find highest rated products on Amazon and contact your local suppliers, manufacturers, importers to get the product on a 45- or 60-days credit, you even don't need to pay anything before you make a sale, just to pay smaller debts. Then you can increase number of sales by driving some traffic through affiliate sites such as coupon sites, cash back sites, classified sites, fever gigs, Facebook ads, Amazon marketplace ads, etc. You can pay off any amount of debt using this small but highly effective strategy if you don't know anything else.

5. Find a product or service or program which has higher margins than 60% or 80%.

6. Know your buying price and net profit after all taxes.

7. Know how many sales you need to make to pay off your first smallest debt and add few extra sales.

8. You are done. Start paying off your debt free.

Once you fill in the above list, below are some **rules of debt** that you can follow to attain financial freedom.

Rule #1—Never pay bad debt with your own existing earned money. Instead think about a business you can start to earn the money to pay off the debt. Pay your debt using FREE money.

Rule #2—Pay in EMIs: by doing this, you can make lower than what you expected or higher than what you expected. But no matter the case, always pay your debts in EMIs—the smallest or the most important first.

Rule #3—Add one or two products every month to the exiting range, and one or two in a new category to clear debts using the growing deeper and wider formula.

Rule #4—Pay the smallest debt first.

Rule #5—Pay the minimum due amount for higher debts if they are causing penalties or higher interest rates.

Rule #6—Whenever you get your salary, do not pay off debt first. Instead add a product to pay off bills and debt.

Example: If you were originally re-selling mobile phones on the online shopping site, you can go deeper into this by selling more varieties of the same category of phones, or you can go wider by adding things like chargers, earphones, etc. to the mobile phones. It's easy to sell today without talking to anybody.

Rule #7—Manage your credit score. Pay off your dues on time and fulfil your financial commitments with financial institutions to ensure that you have a high credit score for future deals.

Rule #8—Don't count a debt in your income.

How to get more of good debt?

Good debt will help you to maximize passive and portfolio income through investments. There are several ways to get more good debt. But before that, it is important to understand what good debt really is.

Good debt = Lowest interest rate + High income generation

Sources of good debt

1) Banks
    a. Find out the criteria for getting you the loan.
    b. Find out categories of loans where you can get higher debt amount. Examples are personal loan, home loan, top ups, etc.
2) NBFCs (Non-banking financial cooperation)
    a. Find out the requirements to attain a loan from NBFCs. Before you apply, you should always write down the criteria.
3) Peer-to-peer landing
    Based on your credit history, get funding through

local investments or some online platform (which you can Google). There are other ways too, like reaching out to your friends, relatives, local lenders, etc.

How to use debt?

There are certain rules that you must follow when using debt which are highly essential to your financial success.

Rule #1: Do not use a single penny of your debt. Invest 100%. That's the way you are going to multiply it, protect it, and keep it forever.

Rule #2: Invest only in passive income and not portfolio income. This is because fix recurring income is better than something that fluctuates. You have to make sure that you get paid every month before you pay your EMI or interest. Purpose of this investment should be only monthly cash flow.

Rule #3: Never lose this amount—keep that in your mind. Learn to protect and multiply your investments. This money is yours to keep.

Rule #4: Do not confuse debt as your income.

Rule #5: Never save an active debt.

Rule #6: Do not think about spending any sort of debt for one simple reason, you have not earned it.

CHAPTER 10

FINANCIAL DISTRIBUTION PLAN (FIQ)

The art of accumulation of money depends on your distribution strategies. This will change everything in your life, this is what will separate you from the poor and middle class, and will make you start feeling like a millionaire right now. Whenever you receive any amount, your futuristic success depends on how you distribute money you get every time. If you follow this strategy, even if it is not in equal ratio, it will keep you rich forever.

Distributing your money before arrival or on arrival is highly rewarding and it's a great habit to form early in life, and if you haven't acquired this habit you must follow it through and teach your kids as well. This shows your financial intelligence and control over the most difficult game.

You can design your own page or you can also download this from my website. The purpose is to distribute money on arrival and save you from bad times.

Financial IQ

On Date:
_____

Received:
_____

#1. For Secure Investment:	#2. For Active Savings:
#3. To Cover up all Expenses:	#4. For Emergency/Health/ Happiness/Holidays

Year-1>20:10:60:10   Year-2>40:10:30:20   Year-3>50:15:20:15

Note:
_____

_____

REACH
YOUR
DESTINATION

CHAPTER 11

COST OF
FINANCIAL FREEDOM

There are two steps to know what is the cost of your financial freedom and the next step is about moving further in the same direction, putting you on the track of being financially free.

Step 1
Calculate your current total income and cash flow for the next twelve months, fixed and flexible both from your earned income, passive income, and portfolio income.

Write down even if it is very embarrassing for you. It was heartbreaking and supremely embarrassing for me—I felt like slapping myself when I did this sitting in my apartment, analyzing my rock bottom bankruptcy and financial situation (I was going to vacate my flat because I had no money for the rent)—but worth it all in the end. If you haven't been broke, if you haven't suffered enough, if you haven't survived the financial storms, you are not authorized to teach anybody . . . That's why I can teach you how to be financially free. It's okay if your income is less or stopped or stolen or you are stuck, still write it down. You have to be willing to do whatever it takes.

Month	Earned Income	Passive Income	Portfolio Income
January			
February			
March			
April			
May			
June			
July			
August			
September			
October			
November			
December			

Step 2
List all your expenses and liabilities for the next twelve months.

Cost of Freedom = Expenses + liabilities/income

When your total expenses and liabilities equals 8% of your monthly income, you will become financially free and it will become easy if you follow step 3. There are three levels of financial freedom.

Level 1 is 8%

Level 2 is 16%

Level 3 is 24%

Under level 1, you can live your life the way you are living for the next 10-12 months.

Under level 2, you can live your life the way you are living for the next 5-6 months.

Under level 3, you can live your life the way you are living for the next 3-4 months.

Below that you are going to live paycheque to paycheque . . . Or let me be straightforward and say that you will survive a poor life if you don't do something about it now.

If you spend 50%, then you are going to hardly survive this way for the next 30-45 days.

Step 3

Add one asset every month or in every three months to produce fixed income from cash flow exclusively.

Add one asset that can make you an income every month. This income must be the difference between level 1 or 2 or 3 to your current spending ratio. For example, if you are spending 50% of your income and you wish to get down to level 3, which is 24%, then you must add 26% (50-24) income in your currency. If you are earning $2000 every month and are spending $1000 but you need to spend $480 (24%) that means you need to earn an extra $520 in profit by following step 3.

CHAPTER 12

STICK AROUND RULES OF MONEY

If you really and truly want money to stick around then you must follow these rules, and if you are stuck somewhere, then read this book again.

Rule #1: Whatever you make, keep 100% of your earned and investment income.

The income that you have earned is yours because you have worked hard for it: you have invested your energy, the most expensive currency of all time. We never spend time on anything: we spend our life. Life is made of mini-micro seconds, when we spend time on anything it's like giving our life to it, if not all then at least a small part. The amount of physical and mental efforts that go in are tremendous and you own the right of that income. You deserve to be paid and keep all of it without any approval. Whatever income has been created by you is a reward of your smart efforts and strategies, so you must find the ways to keep it.

Rule #2: Invest and save before you spend.

Your behaviour controls your financial destiny. I have observed the behaviour patterns of lower-, middle-, and upper-class people, and those who are financially free. In doing so, I have found a huge difference and lots of loopholes. I ran a few surveys on spending and have seen it face-to-face as well. Whenever people get a paycheque or receive money from other sources, they directly head to shopping malls in India. All humans are bound with feelings, emotions, love, affliction, responsibilities and their behaviour pattern is also the same, regardless of their location. What people usually do is that they spend instantly and then they are left with almost nothing. That's the whole story, as I analyzed.

Behaviour pattern of broke, poor, or people with not enough money is:
They earn → spend → not have enough money to survive for the next few days or saved for next two or three months maximum.

Behaviour pattern of middle-class people is:
They earn → spend → save some → invest a little in stupid things or moderately needed → need to earn more to keep up further.

Behaviour pattern of highly rich or wealthy people is:

They earn → invest → save → spend → investment earnings → more earnings from add on sources or existing ones → enough money to live comfortably for generations.

Rule #3: Focus on Assets

A simple definition of an asset is: *money, which comes to your bank account without you working for it.* It can be done if you only decide to work for financial freedom instead of money. An example of generating money without much effort every day is asset management companies, banks, and NBFCs.

You need to learn how these financial institutions perform functions with other people's money. One major thing I can tell you is that they put all their money here and there to generate monthly cash flow for years ahead . . . and protect their investments with legal agreements with the customers.

Second thing is that a bank never loses money under any circumstances. A bank will approach you or you will approach them to open an account. You will have to maintain a minimum balance and if you don't, then the bank will deduct some amount as a penalty. In the second case, they make money directly from the debt, which you have given them: it is the balance in your account. In the first case, if you maintain a balance then they will invest or loan the same amount on a higher interest rate (12%-18%) while you will only get paid 5%-7% annually, and which is way less than the average inflation rate.

Third point: almost any business can be turned into an asset if you think hard enough to find the way. I have analyzed most profitable businesses and their way of generating assets.

Car lease: many big companies purchase cars on EMI and lease it to smaller companies or individuals at a higher rate of interest. This way, they can pay the EMI and also make a profit out of leasing the car. More the assets your company owns, more it is worth and more you can get from the banks and again you can use it to build your company portfolio. It's a cycle and only top successful people are aware of or capable of leveraging everything.

Amazon Prime: Amazon Prime uses limited resources in the form of online content and makes money from their millions of subscribers. Each subscriber pays a subscription fee and utilizes the content. However, Amazon Prime makes a huge profit from this.

Uber: Similar to car leasing, Uber also purchased cars on EMI and gave it to drivers for a higher interest rate. The drivers also have to a pay a part of their daily income to Uber. In this way, the company makes profits on two levels and hence uses limited resources to make unlimited income.

Therefore, an asset is made by providing limited resources to unlimited users.

Great news is that you can turn almost anything into passive income. Other easy and simple examples are rent business, be it property, be it TV, AC, fridge and any other appliances, furniture, etc.

Rule #4: Never buy anything that will depreciate in value until and unless it's not about your life.

Rule #5: Never use debt to pay off another debt. This is the worst-case scenario.

People borrow money for different reasons:

- To finance education, rent a car, medical emergencies (good borrowing).
- For luxuries like expensive clothing, trips, meals (bad borrowing).
- Borrowing to pay off debt (worst kind of borrowing).

  When people borrow to pay off debt, they go into deeper debt and face double interest payments, penalties and get stuck in this race. Soon it becomes a big pain. Think about it like this: borrowing money is a type of spending. If you continue with financial habits that lead to bad borrowing, you will face big trouble like I did. This is because borrowing puts you into problems in the first place and makes you lazy at some points.

The Wrong Way To Borrow

- Attitude:
  - What kind of mentality drives your financial decisions?
  - Why do you spend the money that you spend?
  - Why have you allowed yourself to go into deeper debt?
  - Impulse buying: is it because you could not control your impulses and bought things that you did not really need?
  - We want to be responsible and make solid financial decisions but we have moments of weakness where we overspend and rely on too much credit. To control these wrong ways to borrow, we must keep our attitude towards financial planning in check.
- Savings:
  - You should always aim to save a significant percentage of income and remember to save in gold.
  - Build up an emergency fund so that you do not have to turn to credit in times of emergencies.
  - If you cannot find significant savings every

month, then you are probably heading towards painful situations.

- Budget:
  - o Make a budget that dictates how much of your income goes towards certain items each month.
  - o Making a budget is the only way to get a realistic sense of what your means are, for a short time at least.

Rule #6: Plan ahead of time.

There are two types of people:

- Those who swear by their financial plan
- Those who do not have one

  Without a financial plan, it can be a lot more difficult to reach your goals because you do not know which goal to work on. A financial plan gives you the financial steps you need to take in your life. The following are the essentials of a financial plan:

- Creating a timeline to help you follow your goals
  - o This helps you focus the way you manage money and time on reaching your financial goals.
- Creating a budget
  - o This helps you plan how and when to spend money, save money, and get out of debt.

- Setting your goals
  - When you first prepare your financial plans, you need to have clear goals in mind. The more specific the goals, the better off you are.
  - If you want to retire early, you need to have a an amount that you need to save in order to reach your goal till a specific age.
- A financial plan helps you prepare for big events.
  - Unless you plan for it, you will not be ready to purchase a home, car, or whatever it is you desire
  - For a house, you need to save up for a down payment and clean up your debt so that you can afford the house on time without thinking about a liability or an asset.
- A financial plan helps you to take the steps you need in order to take care of your family.
- A financial plan lets you sleep peacefully because of thought clarity about what you want.

A financial plan can be fluid and change as your dreams and goals change. However, your goals should be realistic. Creating a plan is the first step, you will need to create a budget and break down your goals into manageable pieces so that you can reach them. Create an effective financial plan through careful planning but also commit to following it. This plan will help you take major financial decisions in each stage of your life. Thus, plan ahead of time and pursue your dreams.

Rule #7: Acquire one skill or master one skill in every 2-4 months.

If your goal is to become successful, then you need to have a handful of skills. So, if you plan on learning a new one and dedicating your time to it, you should probably do some research first before deciding. You should also decide if this new skill is going to make you money or it will be some kind of a hobby to make you feel happy. Before deciding, you should also consider how much time of your day you will spare for learning this new skill that will eventually help you become successful.

If your desire is to learn a skill that will make you richer, there are tons of those kinds of skills. But they need more time to master. For example, you can dedicate your time to coding, digital marketing, public speaking, or multimedia design. You can even consider starting to write or focusing on filming and video production. You can master them if you are patient and persistent and focus your time on it every day.

On the other hand, there are skills that will directly impact and contribute to your day-to-day performance and productivity. Such skills are, for example, learning problem solving, relationship building, or health improvement and maintenance. You can even start learning teamwork, self-confidence, self-belief, strategic and creative thinking, and ability to adjust and pivot. Others even concentrate on the ability to focus or open-mindedness.

Even though there are different types of skills, it is essential to **master one skill every 2-4 months in order to not only increase your daily productivity but also to be successful.**

Rule #8: Raise your standards in daily life.

There are so many keys to success but how you feel, how you talk, how you walk, how you look, how you smell, how you maintain your body, how you eat, how you feel, how you act, how you think, how you make decisions, how you plan, how you manage your time, how you distribute your energy on progressive activities and some other equally important factors will have a huge impact on your success if you commit to be world-class. If you look like one soon you will be one, not just physically but also mentally.

Rule #9: Never increase your liabilities without building a steady income with some buffer.

The one concept that links liabilities to income is the net worth of an individual. Net worth is the difference between the value of what you own—your house, retirement funds, investment accounts, checking account balance, etc.—minus such liabilities as the mortgage, credit card debt, and so forth.

Net worth = Assets (at market value) – Liabilities

If you increase your net worth, this means that you have a steady income and can hence increase your liabilities gradually. There are some steps to increase your net worth:

- Review your liabilities: Take a detailed look at your liabilities. Are there liabilities that you can eliminate or reduce? Reducing your debt is a big step in increasing your net worth.

- Review your assets: You may not know exactly how much all of your assets are worth, or how that value is going to change, but you can get a ballpark figure and find out a way if the cash flow can be increased further.

- Trim expenses: Look at your current expenses and find ways to cut back. Because, the less money you spend, the more you are accumulating in net worth. Even a few rupees or dollars can make a difference over the period of a year.

- Reduce debt: This is one of the best ways to increase future wealth by paying off your debt or multiplying debt to generate more income and cover all debts more comfortably.

- Pay off your mortgage: Owning your home is the

biggest asset. Hence, pay off your mortgage to get the biggest liability off your books. Acquire a new skill and pay it off with an extra income source.

- Review annual costs: Your annual costs are bringing your net worth number down; see which ones you don't need. Take a look at things like your loans, insurance, and healthcare premiums each year. Compare interest rates and see if any of these annual costs can be trimmed down anyhow.

- **Income investing:** For income investing, you can use the 'Cash Flow Driven' method. With this approach you only invest in businesses or items, which can provide you monthly cash flow; if something can't give you a steady monthly cash flow, then step away. It's not for you at all because we are investing for financial freedom here.

Rule #10: Be mentally rich.

To be mentally rich you have to develop a mindset around what you want and where you want to be. You must be highly resourceful, skilled, knowledgeable, informative, and careful with the right attitude towards money because it sticks only with people who don't waste it and love it like anything. I recommend my best-selling book *Money Mining Habits* to develop a rich mindset; I have mentioned more than two hundred rich personality traits for you.

Rule #11: Work for financial freedom.

To understand this rule, you should personally answer the following questions:

Do you want to live more? Why?

_____

_____

_____

Do you want to work less? Why?

_____

_____

_____

Do you want to reduce stress?

_____

_____

_____

Financial freedom is when your income exceeds your expenses. In such a case, you have free time, money, and energy to invest into learning other skills, developing products, and perhaps even increasing your income streams.

- **Living more:** There are some who like to work. They feel energized every morning by the idea of getting something done. They like their co-workers. They enjoy serving their customers through a system or high-end behavioural and service delivery protocols and they can't see themselves not working. They like to earn money. They feel the happiest when they work hard but also love to play hard. They would rather have less time off but splurge on the things that make them happy. They might want to live large and enjoy the finer things in life. If this sounds like you, you need to make sure that you have a plan to maintain this great lifestyle throughout your life. Many of you tend to spend too much. Once you reach retirement age and decide to slow down a little bit, you will probably want to continue this lifestyle and will need a large amount of assets to supplement your income. So why not start living your desired life now, or a year later, once you are financially free?

- **Working less:** There are some who are not fulfilled at work. They would rather spend time with loved ones. They like a simpler life. To them, relationships are what are most important. They would like to find a way to not need to work for money, They are not interested in status and getting more stuff; they know that life is short, and they want to live in the moment. They are more interested in life experiences than anything else. If this sounds like you, you need to be able to get rid of any expense you don't really need.

Being thrifty will enable you to reach your goal fast. If your needed income is lower, you will reach financial freedom that much faster and the road to financial freedom will be easier.

- **Reducing stress:** Many don't really know if they'll ever be able to retire. They might stress over money. They don't really know what to do. They don't know if they are on track to reaching their goals, and even the thought of looking at their statements stresses them out. To them, freedom could mean feeling better about themselves. To know that they will be okay. If they were able to be ready for anything that could happen to them, life would be so much simpler and better.

To be financially free one doesn't have to wait for years. It is way easier than fighting for two years of regular income in the corporate world if you follow the above-mentioned rules and rest of the book content. It is harder for those who are afraid of a change in life. I would say, "Don't shut the door on the only opportunity which has the keys."

CHAPTER 13

CHANGE YOUR PERCEPTION OF MONEY

This book is all about practical steps towards financial freedom and on the way to financial freedom there are some hard obstacles, which are either mental or financial. We have to break our old belief system by replacing it with something which has worked for the topmost millionaires and billionaires. You should always praise and appreciate other successful people because they deserve it, and it's a successful habit that we are forming, installing in our brain.

I want to let you know that it's our perception that makes us feel the way we feel about anything and everything. Think about the Apple brand; they want you to think of them as the best, finest, premium brand. By asking you to 'think differently' they position themselves as an exclusive ultimate innovation company in the world, and they do it through all their advertising, marketing, branding, PR activities. Think a bit harder now: the perception which you have of Apple will make you buy an iPhone or not? If you are offered an LG or a Samsung handset, would you buy that? Why not? But there are people who will buy LG and Samsung as well because those brands have also controlled the perception of a different market segment. So, what's really the point here? It is that **you will get anything based on your perception**—if your perception towards money is right then you will get the money but you have to create your own perception because money is not a product of any particular company so it becomes your own duty.

First of all, to create your perception towards money, you have to terminate misconceptions. I won't be listing all the misconceptions but the major ones which have a stronger impact on your success.

Money cannot buy happiness

Think of Yuvraj Singh, the famous Indian cricketer who suffered from cancer. Did he not use money as a resource to buy treatment, and hence indirectly buy happiness for himself and his family? You can Google Yuvraj Singh Cancer story, look at his images and videos of that time, and you will come to know how money can buy you happiness and if it can't buy you happiness then I guarantee anybody on this planet that lack of money will buy them a miserable life.

In my social life, I believe in three basic principles:

→ I will help people get a cure for life-threatening diseases and not let them suffer because of lack of money. I just can't see children dying in hospitals or in rural areas because they couldn't afford the best treatment. How inhuman!

→ I will help people get jobs by generating more job opportunities to feed thousands or millions of families and make them happier.

→ I will help someone pursue their dreams. For example, if someone wants to be a sportsperson, but lacks funds, I will sponsor them. Now imagine if you help somebody to become more successful, wouldn't that bring happiness to that person and his family and maybe to the whole nation almost, and maybe that success can create a huge impact on a thousand or million more lives, who knows? It's a chain of good karmas, which we must create without expecting anything in return.

Therefore, **happiness can be bought with freedom and with money.**

IF YOU THINK MONEY CAN'T BUY YOU HAPPINESS THEN YOU ARE SHOPPING AT THE WRONG PLACES.

I personally believe that money should be used to change the lives of people rather than just kept or used for wrong, criminal purposes.

Think about this really hard: if you do not have money to fulfil your dreams, buy the things you want, eat what you like, and travel where you wish to, will you be happy?

Money is the root of all evil

It is not money but poverty that is the root of all evil. This is because poverty actually leads to higher rates of crimes, murders, and rapes. Think about the number of people who are in jail—most of them are from poor background. There are two reasons for this:

- The rich are out on bail because they can afford lawyers, etc. to take care of legal cases.
- Poor people are the ones committing more crimes because they need a ready source of income for their daily needs.

There are so many negative misconceptions about money, if I start writing I will have to add hundred more pages, so let's just focus on building your positive perception about money if you really want to be financially free.

Money is simply a measurement of the scale of success, knowing who is doing more in life, who is impacting the economy and lives of millions here and there. Our world is on sale, everything has a price tag, whatever you want or need you have to buy and pay the price. If you don't have enough money then you have to settle for less or nothing at all and you will lose out on the greatest opportunities which could have made you millions.

#1. Money can buy you freedom.

Freedom is an experience, just like sitting in a Ferrari. Money gives you the power to move around, stay at a five-star hotel as long as you want, and whenever you want.

If you have enough money, you can hire the best lawyers, accountants, advisors, consultants, and have your people in the system to control your interests.

#2. Money can buy you security.

Money is a truly powerful tool to live your life as you wish. You can buy highly impactful security tools to protect you physically (hire bodyguards, Z+ security, exercising, the best cars, etc.), psychologically (by hiring top consultants, advisors), financially (by hiring world-class investment advisors, members), spiritually (holidays, retreats, etc.). Also, enough cash will ensure your success and positioning in your business and unstoppable cash flow even during the next financial crisis.

#3. Money can buy you a new life.

Money allows you to wrap up in one place and start over a new life in other city or another country of your choice. Money gives you buying power and that power is huge. When you have money, you can even buy a Green Card in USA at $900,000+ and settle down there to start a new life, new business, and find a beautiful partner. Almost anything is possible with the power of money. If you have bought a Range Rover and by any chance you meet with an accident on highway, you have 99% chance of survival, hence it can buy you a new life. This has happened with me so I know it better than any other person on this planet.

#4. Money can buy you privacy.

The world is becoming more and more accessible and transparent day-by-day and it is difficult to find privacy if you are rich and famous.

Privacy is a luxury and that's why celebrities and other rich people spend tremendous amounts of money in order to keep themselves out of the focus. When you are rich you become a target of evil people who want to rob you or sneak on you so they can use it for their purpose to make money or becoming famous, whatever it is.

#5. Money can buy you a positive image.

People have opinions, opinions are controlled by perception, and perception is controlled by stories, and stories are covered by the media. The weapon of media is content and content is of four different types which creates buzz and controls billions of lives through text, image, video and audio. If you are rich, you can control all that and have media to cover your visits, messages, launches, events, donations and more to build a good reputation, and positive image, which will be fruitful in order to gain future projects.

.

#6. Money can buy you peace of mind.

A big bank balance and cash flow allow you to live your life on your terms without compromising in life without having to worry about tiny issues like paying bills, paying school fees, buying medicines, etc.

When you have money, you are calm, comfortable, and composed to take full advantages of any opportunity coming your way, but when you are poor you have no other option than to let it pass and your whole family faces the consequences of that decision.

#7. Money can buy you comfort.

Money can make your life incredibly comfortable and stress-free. You can have everything as per your standard protocols and luxurious lifestyle. You can get rid of unnecessary struggle and pain. Live within your comfort zone and you will be more productive, you will make wiser decisions, you will start taking actions well before time rather than trying to manage loan or mortgage payments; you will start working on shaping your future.

#8. Money can buy you health.

One of the best experiences is feeling healthy. People who are super productive know how important it is to stay healthy. A healthy mind resides in a healthy body.

Money allows you to buy the best memberships for swimming, gymming, dancing, karate, spa, salon memberships, and everything else. Having more money in your bank account gives you access to almost anything and everything in the first place. When you have enough money, you can buy life-saving medicines, and the best health supplements. You can also afford to pay a celebrity fitness trainer and come out with a six-pack body in six weeks. That is the power of money.

#9. Money can buy you confidence.

Confidence is about how you feel about yourself, how you look at other things, and how you react. When you have millions in your bank account, you stop caring about what people would think of you, how they will perceive you, because what people think about is none of your business anymore.

More cash in your wallet will change the tone of your voice, your walk and your style. If you don't believe me then carry $1000 or $5000 in your back pocket and walk on the road, instantly you will find the psychological connection. I have done that and I still carry the same amount. Go give it a try and give me your feedback. Write to me.

#10. You can buy time.

Stupid people would always tell you that you can't buy time with your money but do you know that buying time is the number one skill of top CEOs, MDs, and entrepreneurs.

Let me explain. Look at any millionaire or billionaire in this world. They have outsourced work which they could do easily at a small-scale or maybe on a large one, but they hired others to do it in exchange of money as a fees or salary.

If you want to be successful then you must adopt this concept of buying time, it is as important as generating a huge cash flow, raising funds or making profit. Buy time for your richness and while money does what it is supposed to do, you focus on bigger goals, your vision for your life, your company, and the legacy you wish to leave behind. Remember, a legacy lives forever and it can be only created if you have more time, more hands, and more brains for your success.

#11. Money can buy you pleasure.

Money can buy pleasure and most of the time happiness is in pleasure, whether it is a good situation or a bad one because that demands how you process things in your mind.

#12. Money can buy you big toys.

Money can buy you the topmost luxury cars or a private jet or a big house somewhere in the woods or on the beach. Enough money makes everything easily affordable.

#13. Money can buy you more money.

Why do the rich get richer and the poor get poorer? The rich know how to use their money find a highly profitable opportunity/opportunities and squeeze maximum profits out of it, which is buying money ultimately. Money buy in an opportunity is the secret of insane wealth.

Another thing to mention is that rich people just don't use their own money to buy more money but they also use other people's money, which is called the 'OPM' method. That is why rich people are never afraid of taking huge debts/loans because they know how to make it an asset and generate free cash to buy more money. It becomes a never-ending process and the rich get to keep more than 100% of debt of which they have taken even after paying it 100%.

#14. Money can buy you a legacy.

Poor people work for money or trade their time for money or things because their time equals to money, but the real big ones have a vision and their time equals to their vision. You can have a vision for yourself, for your family, but if you wish to earn your name in history you need to work to create legacy, and that is the biggest vision one can acquire. Another thing which matters is how serious you are about creating your legacy. Look at prime ministers, vice presidents, venture capitalists, who have reached the top of the world but are spending their money to create a legacy for themselves. **A new currency is attention to problems and abilities to solve them at any cost**. This also goes for ministers who are on the patch to create a legacy by making the right decisions for their own people or for the entire humanity. Remember, a person dies thrice: first time is when you stop working on your dreams or give up on life, second when you are in your grave, and the third when the last time somebody mentions your name.

It's your time to decide what you want to work for? How you want to be remembered?

CHAPTER 14

REASONS FOR FINANCIAL FAILURE

Why are you not making money?

Financial freedom is inherently dependent on only one factor: the direction in which you are heading. Every wrong decision will put you off track and every wise decision will bring you closer to your financial independence.

If you fail to focus on your day-to-day result-oriented activities and are distracted all the time, you will not be successful, and hence financially free.

If you fail to manage and distribute your money well, you will not be successful and hence financially free.

If you fail to work on your long-term goals and be passionate about the things you love to do, you will most definitely not be successful and hence financially free.

You can move in the right direction because all the major tools have been provided to you. You might face different situations than I did but ground rules will be the same for those who are ready mentally for financial freedom.

This chapter talks about the reasons for financial success or failure. Why majority of people fail and why some succeed? It is interesting to see that the parameters and factors that influence financial freedom are the same. The starting point of financial success is the same but majority of people take a random direction and land on the dry financial desert. Whether it is self-esteem, energy, or motivation—the lack of this factor will lead to failure and hence deter an individual from attaining financial freedom. If you have high self-esteem, you are energized and motivated to do your work, then you will be successful and attain financial freedom. The way you think, react, and behave in a situation makes all the difference between success and failure. Do you want to be successful and financially free or do you want to be a failure and financially stuck? The ball is in your court.

Reasons for Failure and Success are the same

It can be said that if you focus too much on attaining success, this will just remind you of all the things you do not have. But rather, if you are not deterred by failure and take challenges head on, you might just succeed because the moment you decide to take any challenge on the way to an unknown or known journey, you become unstoppable. Let us look at a simple example to understand this. If you want to lose weight to become healthier, you will focus on the fact that you are in fact overweight and unhealthy at the moment. Instead, if you start taking action and are not affected by the hurdles in your way, you will most definitely be on the path of attaining the healthy body you dream for. You don't see the pain in the process, all you can see are the end outcomes, feelings, emotions, respect you are going to welcome in your life after all those big or small but meaningful achievements.

Measuring success or failure is not simple and it depends on each individual and their definition of those terms. However, there are certain parameters that either aid or deter success and failure. The reasons for success and failure are almost the same because if the parameters are positive, you attain success and if the parameters are negative, you attain failure. For example, if you are energetic and positive about your dreams and passions, you will definitely attain success. On the other hand, if you lack energy and are negative towards your goals, you will be on the path to fast failure. Energy is one of the prime factors which majority of failures ignore, and then wonder why they have failed. **Your energy turns into excitement, and excitement turns into love with your goals, and goals turn into daily progressive momentum and daily progressive momentum turns into your desired results . . . just remember that most people confuse this progressive momentum as activities, which is a waste of time—stay away from the activities which are not progressive, which**

will not produce any results today. You can break your success journey in few steps and simply measure any goal by checking out whether you are making a daily progressive momentum or not.

Financial success can be defined as having stability and a good amount of expendable income. On the other hand, the absence of the above can be defined as financial failure along with debt, etc. Thus, the factors that cause a person to be financially successful can also cause them to be financial failures. The difference is the way in which individuals handle these factors. It took me a while to understand how to handle money, but once I learnt, there was no going back. Once you taste success and get a hold on your money, nobody can take that control away from you. You must remember one thing and pass this on to people you love most.

Money which you pay to anybody in any form whether it is a payment, bill, or tax, is not just the money, it's your life!

Let me expand on this a bit. Money is an outcome of your mental, emotional, physical, spiritual, or social efforts, and those efforts required time. Time is counted in seconds, seconds are hours, hours are days, days are years, and years are life because your life is measured in years. So be extremely wise with your money.

Let's get back to more reasons for financial failures and disasters:

1. **Delay in decisions**

   When you know that something will make you financially stronger and yet you keep adding time, keep delaying the necessary action steps. This is a guarantee that you will reach your financial destination late and will never be financially free. **If not NOW then WHEN?** That's a million dollar question to ask when you delay your decisions. Just decide not to add any more time, and do whatever it takes to become successful.

2. **Not having a quality product**

   You can be working really hard but the quality of your product gets you a refusal from a client; this might be a reason in a few cases. Never forget that the quality of your product must satisfy the need of your clients.

3. **Less market demand**

   If you are trying to sell a product which has no or very less market demand then there is no way that you can be rich or even think about financial freedom. There must be enough demand of your products and you should reach out to your clients before others.

4. **Marketing to the wrong market**

   Sometimes, the major reason of failure isn't a faulty/wrong product but marketing your product to the wrong market segment. What happens is that you waste too much time, money, effort, and get in a deeper loss. Decide about the right market. You must make profit, profit, and only profit to grow rich and become financially free.

5. **Marketing at the wrong time**

   One shocking reason of failure is marketing your product at the wrong time when you are about to get lowest returns on your investments.

6. **Product has tiny margins**

   Tiny margins eat up on your potential and decrease the chances of financial freedom. It is extremely hard to market a product which has lower margins than its marketing and operational cost, unless you don't up-sell, cross-sell, or down-sell products with a high conversion rate.

7. **Selling less in quantity**

   If you are still not making money despite having the perfect product, it means you are not selling it in enough quantity. You are not making enough profits to become financially free.

8. **Fear of failure**

   Fear of failure is primarily caused by a lack of knowledge. If an individual does not know how to drive a car, he is going to be afraid of accidents. Thus, it is simple to understand that in order to get rid of the fear of failure, it is essential to gain knowledge. Once an individual has information about the topic, he will not be so afraid anymore.

Fear of failure is also inherently human nature. Imagine if you are strolling in the jungle and come face to face with a tiger, what is your first reaction going to be? Obviously, you will run! It might not save you from the tiger, but it is what you will do to protect yourself. This is the flight or fight response. **Whenever an individual is faced with a problem, he undergoes a mental analysis and decides between fight or flight.** The problem arises when you do not run in the face of danger, in this case the tiger, and stay stuck in your position for him to attack you. This is a negative response to a problematic situation. Now imagine if you are armed, you are with a group, and you all have guns. How fearful are you going to be? Now imagine another situation where your baby is next to that tiger. Will you be afraid to fight? I am sure I will fight even though I know I might die because the life of my baby is more valuable to me than the fear of fighting a tiger. My question is how can you give up on your baby? Your business is your baby, your dream is your baby, your family is your baby, and that tiger is just the fear. Act despite of the fear to save your baby and live the life you truly deserve. And if you don't act . . . you don't deserve it.

Every action always has a reaction. If you do not work today, you will be putting your future goals at risk. An employee or even a business owner has to put in efforts on a day-to-day basis in order to attain the goals they have set. It is, thus, important for them to have a positive response to every problematic situation. For example, a sales person has certain targets that he has to achieve by the end of the month. If he does not do the required meetings on a daily basis, he will not be able to meet that target and will have hence failed. People who do not achieve targets in a company are thrown out; in life you are rid of all the comforts, and life makes you suffer like anything.

9. **Lack of self-confidence**

Self-confidence is that little thing that makes a big difference. The distinction between someone who is confident and who is not can clearly be seen in the way they carry themselves, talk, and behave. If you are not confident enough, you will never be able to focus on your dreams and reach the pinnacle of success. If you are looking for ways to develop your self-confidence, look no more!

Here are five powerful ways to boost your confidence, which have been super powerful for me personally:

1. **Stay away from negativity**

○ Stay away from the people who silence your personality; these are control freaks and make you feel inferior; you can never grow till you are with them.

o   Evaluate your inner circle, including friends and family. Seriously consider getting away from those individuals who talk rubbish, talk about people, events, and situations you have nothing to do with.

o   Be positive and put some positive enthusiasm into your interactions with others and hit the ground running. Use exciting, charismatic, rare, meaningful words in your conversation and make it about the person you wish to talk to.

o   Stop focusing on the problems in your life and instead begin to focus on solutions and making positive changes.

2.   **Change your body language and image**

o   The simple act of pulling your shoulder back gives others the impression that you are confident.

o   Smiling will not only make you feel better but also make others feel more comfortable around you.

o   Maintain eye contact, speak slowly and clearly while having a conversation to ensure that you emanate self-confidence.

o   Dressing well makes others perceive that you are successful and self-confident, so take some time to create and manage a good outer appearance as well.

3. **Do not accept failure**

o **Never give up. Never accept failure. There is a solution to everything.** Make this your new mantra because succeeding through great adversity is a huge confidence booster.

o You become what you preach inside your head. Thus, switch negative reactions to failure to a positive reaction until you are confident enough of dealing with the hurdles.

4. **Be prepared**

o If you are prepared and well researched, you will have the knowledge to back up everything you say and do. This will give you the confidence that you need to succeed.

o Prepare yourself before any opportunity has a chance to show up because it's better to have an opportunity and be prepared rather than having an opportunity in hand and not be prepared.

5. **Be Highly Resourceful**

o Low self-confidence appears in absence of sufficient amount of knowledge. But you can simply change this in the next 30 days in any area of your life. Simply write down the areas where you don't feel confident enough; number two, surround yourself with high quality content: order top 10 books on those areas, watch 100 videos on each topic by top

10 speakers on the dedicated subject; number three, set your twitter feeds, set Google alerts for the same keywords, find top 10 blogs on the same topics and subscribe. Soon you will be an expert on that topic. Once you are full of high-quality information, then you won't hesitate to talk about it anywhere, in front of anybody.

10. Fear of success

The fear of success phobia is very much like the fear of failure: both prevent the sufferer from dreaming and achieving his or her goals. It might seem weird to fear success; after all what can be more appealing in life than success? However, a little bit of digging in the phobic's mind shows that fearing success comes naturally to you, simply because you are not looking for any change. It's an unknown paradise after all and people like known hells better. You are so comfortably numb in your current situation that you want to continue to live the life despite hating it. Often, the individual might be afraid of success owing to the fear of inability to handle fame or the wealth it brings, and you say, oh, my God! What will happen if I become very famous? How am I going to handle the it?

There are some reasons that cause the fear of success:

- Fear of getting what you want and finding yourself unable to handle success in this moment, but let that moment come and you will learn to handle that amount of success. Be open to any amount of success without getting afraid.

- The dread or deep fear of success is usually deep-rooted. A person may be exceptionally talented, yet he or she may have a long list of under achievements. This becomes a vicious circle as he or she refuses to set goals. What you have achieved so far you can achieve more than that, at least ten times more. You create progressive momentum around your dreams, goals, and don't stop for any small or big achievement; be hungry.

- If you are shy, introverted and you do not like being in the limelight, you might suffer from achievemephobia (fear of success). If this is the case then there are great businesses which you can run from behind the curtains, for example you don't know so many CEOs, as they work quietly behind the scenes. Another example is voice over artists. Or you can actually just decide to change your nature, habits, actions, to change your results. Be opposite to this, if this is what is stopping you. Remember your rescue door—HOW?

- Getting ahead of friends, colleagues, and close family members can be intimidating and threatening, one might fear breaking ties with these people. But if they love you, they must love to see you in a better position than themselves, otherwise you should stay away from them as well.

- The fear of success phobia often stems from guilt or self-doubt. Success comes with responsibilities, which can lead to fear. Guilt is fake—nothing is right and nothing is wrong; do not feel guilty at the expense of your dreams, any guilt isn't worth that much.

- A child who has always listened to comments like, "You will not succeed", "You are a loser", etc. might carry the belief well into their adulthood, undermining everything they do. Mark this, repeat this 100 times to yourself that your reality is what you think, not what people think of you or advertise.

There is only one thing that is standing in the way of your success. Can you guess what it is? It is you. It is me. It is us. We set deadlines, create to-do lists, write marketing plans, network like crazy, and tell people about our incredible ideas. Nothing else is in the way of getting us to where we want to go, except self-sabotage—the pesky excuses for why we didn't get something done, telling ourselves mediocre is good enough or believing that the huge goal we set is just too big. This is not because we cannot do the big thing; it is just because we are afraid of the result.

Ask yourselves these questions:

Why am I standing in my own way?

_____

_____

_____

What does success look like to me?

_____

_____

_____

What happens when I am successful?

_____

_____

_____

Why am I standing in my own way?
- Find out all that you have to let go of in order to be successful. Get rid of the bad habits like you get rid of garbage.
- What things have others said that are still firm in your mind?

- Are they positive or are they negative?
- What do you think about yourself?
- Why do you think that you are not being able to succeed?
- What does success look like to me?
- Getting clarity on your goals is the key to knowing what success looks like.
- Success can be a moving target.
- Will you hit a certain monetary goal in order to be successful?
- Do you need to help a certain number of people to feel successful?
- Are there smaller successes along the way that can set you up for the big success?
  What happens when I am successful?
- It can be a huge release to finally be successful, but what will happen when you finally get there?
- Will you set another goal?
- Will you celebrate?
- Will you find a new direction?
- Will you quit?
- Will you start working towards creating your own legacy?
- What is it that you will do? What more? What will you do differently? Just think.

The fear of success is a self-limiting concept that plagues a large number of people similar to the fear of failure. In order to get rid of the fear of success or failure, figure out what is standing in your way and what will happen when you actually cross that hurdle. As mentioned earlier, the parameters to measure success and failure are similar. Thus, use these parameters in a positive manner to ensure that you achieve the success that you deserve rather than staying stuck in one stop and struggling all your life.

11. Not feeling worthy enough

One of the worst reasons that has been holding a lot of good people from being successful is that they don't feel good enough. That's why they don't feel worthy enough. This feeling of not feeling good enough is created out of praising wrong people at the expense of your life, comparing yourself with other highly successful people without knowing their story of struggle, age, circumstances, stupid decisions, mindset, dumb mistakes, hidden secrets, and so on. The feeling of not being good enough affects a lot of individuals and is a huge deterrent to success. Not feeling worthy enough is linked with being under-confident and having low self-esteem. In order to attain success, it is hence important to develop confidence, self-esteem, and motivation, which will indirectly lead to improvement in self-worth as well. Most importantly, stop comparing, complaining, and praising others on your expense.

Here are the 13 ways to overcome the fear of not feeling worthy enough:

- **Find the root of the fear:** Whether this feeling is based on a reality or what we perceive others are thinking about us, finding out the root of the fear is the first step in overcoming it. If we allow ourselves to start feeling the positive things people say about us are true, we will start feeling worthy enough.

- **Fake it till you make it:** If you are not confident, pretend that you are. Confidence is easy to fake—or don't fake it, make it your reality. Build yourself up from within so that you can be confident in the long run.

- **Focus on past successes:** Think about your past successes to help you get over the fear of not being good enough. If you have done it once, you can definitely do it again. Remember what you did to overcome a challenge or achieve a certain goal, replay it in your mind and visualize a successful outcome over and over again. You can repeat the same if you think it will work in the current situation.

- **Expose yourself to the feared activity:** Exposure to an activity that you fear can help alleviate the fear and anxiety around feeling inadequate. If you can overcome something you fear, you can overcome anything. This helps build confidence and self-esteem.

- **Do not use self-deprecating language:** It is time to believe in your words and communicate them to people. Do not think that your opinion is not good enough or smart enough. If you stop deprecating yourself, you will feel more motivated and energized. Praise yourself, tell yourself that you are nice looking, you are beautiful, you are handsome, you are wise enough to overcome any problem. Believe . . . believe . . . believe in yourself, not in others. Start treating yourself with the most respectable language that you want people to use when they speak to you. Appreciate everything about yourself.

- **Be mindful of your body language:** Physical impressions are more important than you realize. Make sure that you are mindful of the way you dress, behave, and present yourself. Once you present yourself confidently, you will inherently begin feeling internally confident too. If you hold your head up, back straight, shoulders a bit tight but comfortable, then you will see the different emotions, feelings going on in your head about yourself, your body language will change the way you feel about yourself and the way people see you.

- **Practice it every day:** The more you practice being self-confident by upgrading your knowledge, self-image, communication skills, etc. the better you become. Make sure that you talk to yourself more positively and surround yourself with people who make you feel confident.

- **Celebrate your successes:** Confidence will turn your thoughts into action, and that action will help you achieve anything you set your mind to. And don't forget to take note of—and celebrate—your successes when they happen. No matter how small your successes are, you should celebrate them. This act can boost your spirit up; it's a habit which we are forming.

- **Figure out what your learning style is:** Everybody has a unique mind, unique way to adopt things, process knowledge, some like videos, some like books, some classroom-style communication, and so on. Research all you can to find out what it takes to get good at what you want to do and make a plan that is realistic. It is better to know what your own learning style is—to take it slow or dive right in—before you begin demeaning yourself for learning differently from others.

- **Remember to love yourself for who you are:** Stop comparing yourself to other people. You deserve to be celebrated for being yourself. Start loving yourself for no reason and for every reason, in your bad moments and in your good times. Your first job is to love yourself and keep yourself happy.

- **Stop overthinking:** Overthinking is toxic and can affect your self-confidence. The power that we hold within ourselves lies beneath all the toxic, useless overthinking. Overthinking creates confusion, and a confused person can't take a clear shot in life, and confusion creates delay in decisions, and delay in decisions will delay or destroy your chances of success.

- **Work on your well-being:** You cannot feel great about yourself if you do not feel great from within. Take time to maintain your health in order to feel good and feel confident about yourself and get rid of the fear of not being good enough. Start working on your physical and mental health every day with discipline and routine.

12. Fear of people

Do you ever stop in the middle of your tracks or before you even get started and think, what will people think about you if you fail? If you do, then you might never be successful. Imagine that you are going for a jog and you constantly think about what others are thinking about you. Throughout the jog, you will stop multiple times to check your appearance in shop windows or use your towel to wipe your overly sweaty face. You might wonder what people think about your body, your clothes, your motivation, and the way you jog. It is almost like you do less jogging and more thinking, defeating the entire purpose of the jog. On the other hand, if you do not bother about what people will think or say, you will actually end up enjoying the jog, and come back refreshed and energized for the day.

This question of what will people think or say about you should not bother you at all. Think about it this way: if you are hungry, are these people going to put food on the table for you? If you want something and you do not have the money to purchase it, are they going to help you buy that? Are these people going to stand by you in your time of need? No! Then why must you bother about what they believe, think or say about you? The first step to alleviate the fear of people is to understand that what others say does not really matter.

What a person thinks depends on their perspective and perception. But, ask yourself this—does another person stop in their tracks when you think or say something? The motivation to achieve something, the passion with which you pursue it has to come from within. As long as you believe in yourself, no thoughts or words can ever bring you down. Remember, finally that what people think about you, will never become your reality but what you think of you will make you or break you; it's never the people.

'**YOU WILL NEVER BE SUCCESSFUL IF YOU DON'T STOP CARING ABOUT WHAT PEOPLE WOULD SAY OR THINK ABOUT YOU.**'

13. **Laziness**

Being lazy can make it more difficult for you to focus on tasks and execute them on time. The one thing that comes with being lazy is procrastination, which makes you delay doing the task that you are supposed to do. For example, if you have an assignment due in a few weeks, procrastination makes you start just the night before the submission. This reduces the quality of work and adds a lot of stress. The assignment could have been well-researched and worked on before had you not been lazy about it. Being lazy will keep you poor or if not poor, then far from your dreams.

There are some simple tips to overcome laziness:

- **Break down a task into smaller tasks:** Breaking a task into smaller tasks, step-by-step, solves the problem of avoiding tasks because they seem so overwhelming. When you break down tasks, they do not seem as intimidating as before.

- **Rest, sleep, and exercise:** Laziness can be owing to exhaustion and lack of energy. You need to give your body the sleep and rest that it needs as well as exercise and fresh air. Load yourself with abundance of energy every morning and the night before with high protein food. Most of the time we don't take any action because we do not have sufficient amount of energy to move.

- **Motivation:** In some cases, laziness is due to a lack of motivation, which can be strengthened through visualization, affirmation, and thinking about the importance of doing the task or achieving your goal. You can read self-help books, watch videos on YouTube, subscribe to motivational blogs, and follow motivational twitter profiles, etc.

- **Have a vision of what or who you want to be:** Frequently reflecting on the person we want to be, the goals we want to achieve, and the life we want to live can motivate us to take actions.

- **Think about benefits:** Think about the benefits of overcoming laziness and doing the task at hand. Do not focus on the hurdles or difficulties because that deters you from taking action. Instead, make a list of the benefits and focus on them while giving your best effort.

- **Think about consequences:** Think about what will happen if you continue to be lazy and do not do the work that you are required to do. One example is that it will pile up and you might never be able to complete this work on time.

- **Doing one thing at a time:** Focus your time and energy on one task at a time to ensure that you do it to the best of your abilities.

- **Visualization:** Visualize yourself achieving the task and imagine how you would feel once you do. Think about the compliments you would receive and the benefits you would get.

- **Repeat affirmations:** Tell yourself that you can do it, only you can do it. Keep repeating positive affirmations to yourself and you'll find a positive change in your mindset.

- **Learn from successful people:** Learn the things that your role models do on a daily basis and follow in their footsteps. The only reason they are successful is because they were not lazy when it came to taking action.

14. Lack of energy

Energy is the lifeblood of our everyday decisions and actions. It fundamentally creates a well-balanced, rounded, and fulfilling lifestyle. Those who are energetic can go through the day being productive, and end up chasing success. But those who are lethargic or lack energy, spend their day whining and complaining, going in the opposite direction of success. However, there are some things that we generally consume or do that create a lack of energy, which in turn deters the possibility of being successful. Change your habits, change your life! I consider ENERGY as the most important part of success. It will keep you going right from the start to the end point; if you have no energy then NOTHING will work, no matter how motivated you are. Ensure you eat, sleep, and exercise in the right amounts to never feel a lack of energy.

15. Being too busy

Being too busy on gadgets and social media is a huge deterrent to success because not only does it cause distractions, it makes an individual work towards an unrealistic dream. People nowadays dream of being social media influencers or gadget gurus. But what they fail to understand is that this is not real life. This will not only push them towards their downfall, it will also be the cause of it.

Why would you want to be a social media influencer, when you can rather be an influencer in real life? Why would you choose to be a gadget guru over becoming famous for your feats? Why would you NOT choose REAL over VIRTUAL? Why would you spend majority of your time reading feeds from the people you even don't like? What if you invest the same amount of time developing your skills?

Just reflect back on what have you gained so far or is there anything more valuable you can achieve if you shift your focus on pursuing your dreams.

16. Being too comfortable

If you are satisfied with a little or with too much, both the situations are dangerous for next level growth—they are highly harmful for your potential, strength, and limits. Success begins at the end of your comfort zone. But if you are too comfortable with where you are, you will not take any action to change your life. **If you don't do something, which you have never done before, you will never get to where you have never been before.** And this in turn leads to a lack of motivation, excitement, and passion.

When you are too comfortable with where you are, you have nothing to work towards. Imagine that you have a big home, lots of fancy cars, and every possible luxury you could need in life. Does this mean that you should not strive for more? Does this mean that you should stay stuck in your perfect life? Perfection is an on-going, ever-changing process. Once you attain perfection, you can always attain something more, something better. If you want to be more successful, step out of your comfort zone, it's hard but highly fulfilling for your success.

There are some psychological struggles that people face when trying to step out of their comfort zone:

- **Authenticity:** When an individual steps out of their comfort zone, they might fear feeling like they are not themselves anymore. The thing to understand is that when you are not yourself, not in your comfort zone, you are more likely to grow and be successful. Don't put yourself too much against your own dreams, success, and wondering what the future holds for you. Have an entrepreneurial spirit and move on; don't hold yourself back at the cost of your dreams.

- **Likeability:** Some individuals fear that they may not be liked when they step out of their comfort zone, and change the way they are. It is not important to be liked; rather it is essential to focus on growth and success. People usually do not like those who are successful, and you can't expect people to like you at every step because people are prone to hating the rich and successful; only other successful people will appreciate you. That's how it is in real life. Do your best to help people you want to do business with; just think about creating value for them, focus on solving their problems, and treat people nicely. People are going to love you instead of liking you, if you do that.

- **Competence:** There are times when an individual feels that he or she is not good enough or competent enough to step out of their comfort zones. Further, they are worried that others will notice that they are not that competent and hence restrict themselves in their comfort zones. Get a grip on your skills, practice a bit more, and step out even if you fail. You can only fail a few times and people who want to be truly successful don't care about any sort of struggle because they know they are bigger than any problem that can appear on the way. Nobody is competent enough in any domain, it's all about how you wish to feel and what you are doing to upgrade your knowledge to help your market better than anybody else. The greater the knowledge you have, the more competent you become. Immerse yourself in the relevant content, analyze your meetings, and pitch better next time.

- **Resentment:** Lots of individuals feel anger, resentment, and frustration that they have to get out of their comfort zone in the first place. For an introvert, talking to other people is the biggest step out of their comfort zones. Thus, they feel resentment when they are forced to have small talk or network with other people. Develop a habit of listening, ask exciting questions, learn new vocabulary, learn the art of talking or automate your system.

- **Morality:** Sometimes, you have to do things that might not be morally right, like firing your own friend from your company, but it is something that has to be done. Morals come into place when stepping out of the comfort zone because it sometimes makes people do things that are against their personal code of conduct. **Excitement:** Excitement is the feeling of elation you get when you are looking forward to something you truly, deeply, and madly love. If you are not excited about your work, you will not think it is fulfilling, and hence you will not attain success easily. Without excitement backing us up, we will never build the habit of working hard on our dreams. Additionally, if we do not start expecting, anticipating, and believing that we will attain our dreams, it will never become a reality. Hence, excitement is the thing that differentiates between someone who thinks and someone who believes. Thinking that you can attain success is good, but believing that you will attain success is much better. For your success, you must have the same kind of excitement as a fan who cheers for his favourite team.

17. Small goals drive fewer miles

If a football game could be won with the first goal, would the players be motivated to even play after the first goal is scored? Although there will be excitement on the field before the first goal, all of this will die out when the goal is scored. The winning team will celebrate and the losing team will leave the field defeated. But now imagine if the game was a traditional game of football. How much excitement would there be on the field! Every player would aim to make as many goals for their own team as possible.

Similarly, in life, small goals only make you work till a certain limit. When you put a limit on your goals and dreams, you put a limit on yourself and the amount of work that you put in. Imagine that you are a writer writing your next novel. If your goal is to write a page a day, will you be motivated or excited to work beyond that one page? No. Imagine that you are a salesperson and you have to make only one sale each day. Will you even think about pitching to another customer after closing the first sale? No. Then, why should you put a limit on your goals when your resources and motivation can be limitless?

18. Unknown ways

Imagine that you are driving in an unknown area and you do not know the way. What are you likely to do? Will you give up and park your car? Will you use Google maps to find your way? Will you ask the locals to help you with accurate directions? The most likely answer is that you will find some way to get to your destination. Similarly, when there are unknown ways or unknown tasks in your path to success, you have to make sure that you find your way around this problem. Whether this means researching more or asking learned people for advice, you have to do whatever it takes to make sure that you attain success.

Just like the fear of failure and the fear of success, the fear of the unknown stems from a lack of knowledge or mentorship. Hence, it is essential for you to figure out the best resources that you can use to fill this gap in knowledge. If you join a new job that requires you to use Excel but you do not know how to because you have never used it before, what is the best thing to do? You could either ask someone who has knowledge to run you through it or watch videos and read articles that simplify the process of using Excel. No matter what, you cannot say that because you do not know, or that you will give up.

19. Negative attitude

People who have a negative attitude about everything, have never succeeded. Everyone has an attitude, but there are differences in the altitude of attitude. Success, hence, depends on the attitude of your altitude. One of the most important steps you can take to attain success is to monitor your attitude and its impact on your work performance, relationships, and people around you. If you have a negative attitude, it will make you see everything negatively. A negative attitude is hence extremely detrimental to success.

Here are 10 strategies to improve your attitude:

- **Self-coaching through affirmations:** Tell yourself that you can do it and cultivate a positive attitude internally. An affirmation is made up with words that have power, conviction, and faith. When you coach yourself with positive words, you drive it into your subconscious which then leads to action.

- **Self-motivation through discovering your motives:** Everyone has a different motivation to do what they do in order to attain success. You can motivate yourself by discovering what it is that you are working towards. Whether it is love, passion, money, etc. you have to discover what it is and keep that central to your identity.

- **The power of visualization:** If you see yourself achieving something, you are more likely to attain it; this is the power of visualization. Imagine that you have already attained whatever it is you want. Behave like you have attained it. Think like you have already gotten it. The power of visualization will make you succeed.

- **Positive internal dialogue:** The little voice that you hear in your head is the one that programs your brain into action. When you positively speak to that voice, you program yourself to attain success.

- **The power of words:** You can create your path to success by what you say, so watch your words. Ensure that you only speak positively because words that are once released into the universe have the power to control outcomes.

- **Positive greeting:** When you start your day in office on a positive note, it develops a positive attitude for a positive life. Make sure you greet those with whom you work to make sure that the positivity in the work place stays intact.

- **Enthusiasm:** This is a burning desire that communicates your commitment, determination, and spirit. Unless you are enthusiastic, you will not be fired into action. Have enthusiasm to celebrate your work.

- **Spiritual empowerment:** Many people find powerful and positive motivation in their faith. Ensure that you channel your spirit and focus on all that which motivates you and keeps your attitude positive, like meditation, yoga, or asanas, etc.

- **Lighten up your life with humour:** The more humour and laughter exist in your life, the less stress you'll have, which means an abundance of positive energy to help you put your attitude into action.

- A sense of doing something positive for yourself with regular exercising makes you feel good about yourself. It hence helps in developing a positive attitude that drives success.

A negative attitude can ruin your own perception of yourself, relationships, and the attitudes of people around you. Hence, stay positive and be successful.

20. Less information about risk

When you take up a hobby, do you not learn everything about the equipment, famous players, and all the jargon you would need to use? Do you not buy all the necessary gear? Are you not completely prepared for this hobby even before you begin? Then why do we not do this when it comes to work and success? Many individuals remain unsuccessful their entire lives because they refuse to learn more about their work: the risks and rewards, the jargon, the tools. Thus, less information is one factor that actually prevents an individual from being successful.

21. Lack of Will like politicians

You want to be successful, but the will to work hard is lacking. Will you ever attain your dreams? If politicians so desire, there is so much that they can do to change the current state of the country. However, the potholes remain on the roads, majority of people do not have access to even very basic necessities like drinking water, quality schools, hospitals, food, electricity, good roads, etc. There is no point in dreaming something if you do not have the WILL to do it. The WILL, the want to do something, is the key to success.

22. Power of the Mind

Our mind is a storehouse of memories, feelings, emotions, and more. Whenever you think about success, your mind visualizes your version of success. Whenever you think about pain, your mind visualizes what pain means to you. The important lesson here is that perception causes a creation of the actual image and success has an image but only a dreamer can see it. If you perceive something to be difficult, the situation, even if it is not difficult, will actually become difficult. On the other hand, if you think about something as easy and doable, it will become easy and doable. Therefore, ensure that you motivate yourself and perceive things in a positive light, which will then make things actually happen in a positive sense.

23. Goals

Unless you have a goal, you will not know what you are working towards. Imagine a football game without a goalpost. Imagine a car on a road without a destination in mind. Imagine a mountaineer climbing up a mountain without defining the summit. Is this possible? No. Unless and until you decide and define your goals, you will be aimless, going round and round in circles. Or worse, you will stay stationary at the point where you are. Having a goal is the first step in attaining success because it is the first step in attaining the goal.

- Have a goal
- Work towards it
- Attain success

Make a dream board with all the things that you wish to achieve and paste it in a place where you can see it every morning. This will ensure that you spend all your time constructively working towards your goals.

24. Planning

Now that you have decided and defined your goals, it is time to plan what you are going to do in order to attain your goals. The plan is the most important thing because it tells you what to do at any given time. Working without a plan is not only messy, it also confuses you. If you do not know what to do when, you might not end up doing anything. Thus, planning is the next step: it is important to ensure that you know what you are supposed to do, and what it is that is going to lead you to as well. Construct a mind map or a table to make a plan that works for you to attain your goals.

25. Routine

Any kind of planning will lead to the creation of a routine. Your routine can be whatever works best for you. But make sure that you put in enough time for work, rest, and rejuvenation, and even exercise. Take timely actions every day to achieve your goals, a very basic routine would look like this.

Time	Task	Comment

26. Unplanned start of the day

Your day always begins at night. If you sleep on time, you will wake up on time to get on with your day. However, if you do not sleep on time, you will not be able to work on your skills, manage your time, and attain what you wish to. If you start your day without a plan, you are most likely going to waste the entire day. When you have a plan, it helps you to work towards your goals, and it also gives you a sense of direction. Thus, in order to attain success and conquer your dreams, always plan your day in advance.

27. Discipline

Discipline is the habit of doing what it takes to attain what you need. For example, if you decide you are going to jog every day for an hour, discipline is when you go jogging each day for exactly one hour without fail. No matter what happens, you do not break this discipline because it showcases that you have conviction as a person. Discipline is created only because of self-control. Unless and until you internally decide that you want to take care of your health and jog for that hour, you will not be determined to actually go ahead and take action.

28. **Dot on growth targets** (find unknown hills)
Potential is unlimited and should not be constricted by certain peaks. Each mountain has multiple peaks depending on the angle from which you are looking at it. Similarly, each individual has multiple opportunities to grow and numerous heights that they can reach. Your potential is only defined by what you do with your knowledge and hence putting a dot on growth targets will actually prevent you from becoming successful, and will halt your growth. It is said that when you cannot dig anymore, then find another spot to dig. Similarly, when you feel like you have reached the pinnacle of success in one field, look for another field to conquer. Multiple skills with limitless potential are what is going to make you successful.

29. Mind your Surroundings

If you want to be a millionaire, start hanging out with millionaires, start listening to millionaires, watching millionaires, and reading about millionaires. If it is not physically possible, then do it virtually.

30. Guard your mind

There are lots of things that can poison your mind. It is important to guard your mind from the negatives and focus on the positives. If you do not take care of your thoughts, there might be cobwebs there after a certain amount of time. The reason is that if you let your mind be affected by negative thoughts, you will eventually become a negative person. Thus, guard your mind to make sure that you only let in the positives, and let your thoughts flow in a good way for great success awaiting you.

31. Mind your own business

Every individual focuses on themselves because they know that they are the most important in their own universe. If you do not mind your own business and do not work on your own agenda, you are just wasting your life. There is a simple technique to ensure that you mind your own business and that is to ask the question:

Whose agenda are you working for?

Always put your benefits first! **If you talk to people when they want to, and there is** no benefit for you in it, then you are on their agenda. If you talk to people when you want to, and you need to, and there is only your benefit involved, then you are working on your agenda. If you talk to people when they want and when you want, that's a mutual benefit, and even then, you are on your agenda.

Therefore, it is important to always work on your agenda first and mind your own business in order to be successful.

32. Lack of resources

People who desperately want to win don't need all the resources to become successful; they can always be more resourceful by reading, studying, watching interviews, taking up professional courses, etc. When you face a lack of resources, make a pros and cons list of using those resources for certain uses. Only then, after analyzing these pros and cons, make the final decision as to where you should use those resources. Lack of resources shouldn't be a hurdle, or an obstacle for not proceeding ahead in life.

33. Faith

Unless you believe in yourself, until you have faith in your own abilities, you will not be on the path to success. Faith is the confidence and trust that you have on yourself to be able to do something. Faith is about figuring out the unknown solution because you have confidence in yourself, and you trust yourself. Imagine that you want to learn how to dance, but you walk into a class claiming that you have two left feet; you will never learn how to dance. Only if you believe in yourself, believe in your ability to learn the art of dance, will you be able to actually learn any dance form that you want to. There are many examples where a little faith has gone a long way.

34. Limited vision of yourself

How successful you really are and how successful you will be depends on how you see yourself. If you see yourself as weak or incapable, you will not be able to attain success. This limited vision of yourself will become a deterrent to success because it will make you feel like you are not good enough. On the other hand, if you have a larger-than-life image of yourself and you see your abilities in a positive light, you are more likely to work harder to gain the success that you believe you deserve. Nothing can stop you from attaining success other than yourself. As long as you believe that you can do it, you actually and truly will be able to do anything that you put your mind to. Have a self-vision on where you wish to see yourself, and how you want people to see you.

CHAPTER 15

WHICH SIDE ARE YOU ON?

After all you have gained from this book, you must choose which side of the economy you are going to stay on. Memorize this table and observe your behaviour all the time; be conscious in making decisions. Your habits create a class in you and being classy is about having a better mindset for success and money at the same time. Your earnings are always equal to or a bit less in comparison to your current productivity level.

Rich	Poor
Take risks	Do not take risks
Face all problems	Avoid problems
Positive focus	Negative focus
Accountability	Blame
Deserve	Claim
Find plus points	Crib
They are strong	Complain
Do not care	Justify
Create opportunity	Wait for opportunity
Invest First	Spend first
Uncomfortable in 'Comfortability'	Comfortable in poverty
Men of action	Men of cares
Bigger than any problem	Smaller than any small problem

Rich	Poor
Appreciate and admire	Pull down everyone
Love sales	Hate sales
Feel worthy	Feel unworthy
Work wisely	Work hard/smart
Open to always learn	Know it all
Prepared before opportunity	Plan to prepare post getting the opportunity
Fast	Slow
Work for greatness	Work for the sake of it
Functional and motivated	Lazy
Improve daily	Wait for the right time
Do not entertain time vampires	Waste too much time on unproductive stuff
Morally successful	Morally unsuccessful
Seek for mentorships or self-taught	No mentors
Growth matters	Survival matters
Believe in networking	Hate networking or do not like to maintain relationships
Sink in listening and respond	Just listen for the sake of it
Do not give up	Give up easily
Forecast future	Afraid of the future
Outsource	Do it themselves
Exercise daily	Do not exercise
Eat healthy	Do not eat healthy
Wake up early	Do not wake up early
Do not check emails	Check emails
Plan day before night	Do as it comes
Time equals vision	Time equals money

Rich	Poor
Love reading	Hate reading
Give back	Try to get more
Do not gamble	Gamble
Mind controlled	Say stupid things without thinking
Mind own business	Mind others' business
Have a routine	No routine
Never use debt to pay off debt	Use debt to pay off debt
Talk about future	Talk about past
Multiple sources of income	Single source of income
Read and study	Refuse to study
Plan ahead	Always unplanned
Purpose driven activities	Activity with no purpose
Live in the moment	Distracted
Manage time well	Pass time
Money brings happiness	Poverty brings sadness
Never limit thinking	Limited self
Have a rescue key – HOW	Have a self-limiting key – Cannot
Have a result	Have a reason
Pay for self first	Pays others
Hungry for more	Satisfied with what they have
Live for legacy	Live for self
Save for good	Save for bad
Spend it wisely	Spend blindly
Net worth driven	Income driven
Do not blame luck	Blame luck

CONCLUSION

———— ▲ ————

Our personality defines us, and our interactions with the world. Personality is shaped by early life experiences and developed over a period of time. It is possible to change your personality by first identifying who you are and then shaping your thoughts, reactions, and behaviours in the way you deem fit. There are essentially three kinds of people—smart, wise and extremely wise—who will have different reactions to the same situation.

One minute overview to *Your Last Step to Fast Financial Freedom*:

- In order to attain financial freedom, an individual has to define their dreams, follow their passions, develop the necessary mindset, and acquire the required skills.
- An individual needs to plan for an income by finding out who can pay them

for the skills they have by recognizing the gap or the needs that they can fulfil.

- To enable an individual to earn and earn more, he or she has to develop their skills deeper and wider, and learn how to manage and distribute their income.

- All individuals need to invest and save before they begin spending their incomes.

- Investing should be mainly in passive income form so that individuals do not have to spend much time, but they can reap the benefits of their investments.

- Individuals should learn that good saving is what makes them money, and that bad saving is what makes them lose money.

- Before spending recklessly, an individual must make a list of all that he or she needs, wants, and can do without.

- To master the debt monster, individuals can make a list of all the debts they have to pay and pay off with the smallest debt occurring first, going in ascending order.

- There are multiple ground rules of money and misconceptions about money that must be understood by each and every individual.

- The reasons for success and failure are the same and have to be acknowledged if a person truly wants to be successful.

- The different types of personalities are shaped by experience and affect the way a person reacts in a given situation.
- You MUST know your cost to financial freedom, and you MUST distribute your income as soon as you get it or in advance.

Aryan Chaudhary is the best-selling author of four books, including *Money Mining Habits*, based on his transformational real-life experiences. A self-made, successful entrepreneur, an emerging thought leader, trusted financial marketing advisor, Aryan is passionate about the financial transformation of individuals and businesses through 'Financial Freedom Marketing' and business growth strategies.